Smart Investors Keep It Simple

Creating passive income with dividend stocks

By: Giovanni Rigters

Table of Contents

Introduction

Ever thought about becoming rich? Want to be your own boss? Want to make passive income even when you're not working? If the answer to all three questions is yes, you might think this is a get rich quick scheme, but that's not the case at all.

One of the best ways to become rich or even wealthy is to study what rich and wealthy people do now and have done in the past to acquire their wealth. Some have inherited their riches, but the majority in today's day and age are self-made millionaires and billionaires.

Look at the Forbes or Bloomberg's billionaire list and you will notice that many of the billionaires have acquired their wealth through their investments.

Just look at the top five (not in any particular order, since they switch positions frequently):

Bill Gates: He became very wealthy with his company Microsoft (**MSFT**), but started a holding company (a company that holds assets, like stocks, bonds, real estate, royalties, and creates subsidiaries for those holdings), called Cascade Investment. The money he made from his company was used to invest in companies such as Republic Services (**RSG**), Four Seasons, and John Deere (**DE**).

Warren Buffett: The Oracle of Omaha also has a holding company, called Berkshire Hathaway, where he invests in and buys companies such as Coca Cola (**KO**), See's Candy, and Proctor & Gamble (**PG**).

Carlos Slim: Mexican business tycoon who has a holding company called Grupo Carso and has made investments in companies such as the New York Times, America Movil, and Phillip Morris (**PM**).

Amancio Ortega: Spanish businessman who started the successful Zara clothing chain and incorporated it into a holding company called Inditex. Afterward, he started investing in various companies and real estate.

Does an investor need to create a holding company to start investing? Of course not, but it is always helpful to know what kind of moves the top guys are making.

These and other billionaires are so influential and powerful that they can single-handedly change the course of business, communities, politics, labor, law, education, health, economics (pretty much every facet of life), whether good or bad.

However, that's not the focus of this book. I'll focus exclusively on investing and try to take something that can be quite confusing and daunting to learn and break it into easily digestible information. I'll show how an investor can get more comfortable and confident with investing and create a passive income stream that will keep the money growing.

Chapter One: Brazen Financial Awareness

I don't have enough money to start investing

We're living in tough times right now, student loans are holding us back, rent keeps increasing and buying a house is also out of the question for many of us.

So you want to start investing, but you either don't have the money or don't know where to start. It does not take that much money to start investing, but most people don't think they can afford to put money aside.

How much do you need to get started? You can start with as little or as much as you can afford. The more you have the better, of course, but if you are drowning in debt (student loans, car payments, rent), you can start small.

If you are hurting for cash, you can start out by buying just **one share** in a high-quality company. Many high-quality companies don't cost that much to purchase just one share. For example, right now an investor can buy one share in Coca Cola for less than 50 dollars.

I'll go into more detail on how to buy shares in companies, but just remember that you don't need to have a lot to get started.

Set up your investment account (we'll talk about this more in detail) to automatically transfer over $20, $50, $100, or whatever you are comfortable with weekly from your bank account. Not only are you **paying yourself first**, your account will also build up and you will be ready to buy investments when the time is right. As you get more comfortable with paying yourself first, you can slowly start increasing the amount you transfer over to your investment account.

You can also just deposit a lump sum in your account, instead of doing automatic transfers, but the benefit of automatic transfers, once set up, is that you'll pretty much forget about it and you will barely notice it making a dent in your lifestyle. Once you get used to depositing small amounts, you can slowly start increasing the automatic transfer amount.

If you can put even $10 a week to the side, after a year you will have $520 saved up, which is a start. You will then be able to use that money saved up to purchase different stocks.

It's best to **start small** because you will be able to mentally bounce back from mistakes you make and losses that will occur. This will also be a good learning experience, which will improve your confidence and analytical skills the longer you invest.

If you start small with let's say the $520, it will give you more flexibility in your thinking and risk-taking than if you started with a million dollars out the gate. You would be too cautious and terrified to make decisions on your own and you would be too scared to lose money.

When you invest you continuously educate yourself. There will be slow times, but there will never be a dull moment.

Why invest in the stock market at all?
The stock market has created many millionaires and billionaires who did not inherit their wealth from their families. This is also where many wealthy individuals park their money and allow it to grow even more.

This market, even with its ups and downs, is still the best market to create and grow wealth that investors will need to live on when they are retired. The stock market also allows money to grow faster than inflation.

What is a stock?
A stock is a share (piece) of a company that you can buy or sell on the stock market. A shareholder is a person or company that owns at least one share of a company's stock.

A stock or share represents **ownership** of a company. If a company has 100 shares and you own 10, then you own 10% of the company.

Most well-known companies, like PepsiCo and McDonalds, have billions of shares outstanding (shares on the stock market), so if you only happen to own 5 or 10 shares in these companies, you only own a minuscule part of the company.

In the past stock certificates, which are legal documents that state the specific number of shares you own in a company, were issued to shareholders. If you wanted to buy or sell your shares, stock certificates needed to be transferred from the seller to the buyer.

This slows down the process of buying and selling, that's why everything now is handled electronically. You can still request a stock certificate, though.

Rumor has it that the very first stock certificate known to mankind was issued by the Dutch East India Company (VOC) in the early 1600s. This certificate is on display at the Westfries Archief in Hoorn, the Netherlands.

Stocks give you the right to vote on the company's operations, you get 1 vote for each share you own, so if you have 300 shares you get 300 votes.

Voting happens once a year and you will most likely receive a message to cast your vote on proxyvote.com

How to make money with stocks
There are four ways to make money with stocks. The most well-known is **buying low and selling high**. This technique involves buying shares at one price and selling it when the share price has increased. The difference is your profit.

So let's say you bought 100 shares in a company for $5 on Monday (which puts your investment at $500) and seven days later the stock price climbed up to $6. Your money (capital) just increased (gain) from $500 to $600.

Now this $100 gain is **unrealized** because your money is still in the stock market and it could either go up or down. You decide to sell and received $600; you just gained $100 in **realized** income ($600-$500).

The second way you can make money is by selling high and buying low, also called **selling short** or going short. With this technique, you borrow shares, sell them at a higher price and then buy them back at a lower price and return the shares you loaned back. The difference is your profit.

For example, shares of a company are trading, which means the process of buying and selling, at $10. You borrow 100 shares of that company's stock and sell these shares for a total of $1000 ($10 x 100 shares). The stock then drops $3 in value and is now worth $7. You buy back 100 shares at $7 for a total of $700 and return the borrowed 100 shares. You just made $300 profit (sold for $1000 – bought back for $700 = $300)

Third, you can make money with stocks buy selling **call options**. With a call option, you give the buyer the right but not the obligation to buy your shares at a **strike price**. For this right, the buyer pays you a **premium**.

For example, you just bought 100 shares in Coca Cola for $38, you then write an options contract, valid for the next 30 days; to sell the shares at a specific price, let's say $40 (strike price).

So this means that the buyer has the right but not the obligation to buy your shares if the price increases to $40 or beyond over the next 30 days. After these 30 days, the options contract will expire. For this right, the buyer pays you a premium of let's say $1.20 per share, so you immediately get $120 ($1.20 x 100 shares) deposited to you.

One options contract always consists of 100 shares. So if you are selling 4 contracts, you are putting 400 shares up for sale.

Now how does this benefit the seller or the buyer? From the sellers' standpoint, you already receive a quick profit from the premium you received, in this case, $120.

Also, if the stock price stayed under $40 for the next 30 days, the buyer will not buy your shares. There is no reason to buy your shares for $40 while the market is selling them for less than $40. So you just made a quick $120 in 30 days.

Now, if an investor did this each month by writing multiple contracts, he or she can start to increase the invested capital fairly quickly.

What happens if the stock increased to $43 within 30 days? More than likely the buyer will use his or her right to buy the shares at the agreed strike price of $40 a share.

In this case, you just made $320 profit, $120 from the premium and $200 from selling your shares at $40 while you bought them at $38 (remember you bought 100 shares).

Now how did the buyer make money? He or she is already -$120 in the hole for paying you a premium, but in those 30 days the stock increased to $43 and the buyer bought them from you at the agreed amount of $40. So the buyer has an unrealized gain of $3 ($43-$40).

If the buyer decides to sell at $43, he or she just made a quick profit of $180. The buyer bought the 100 shares at $40 apiece and sold at $43 which gives the buyer a $300 profit. But the buyer also has to factor in the premium paid, which was $120.

Of course, there are risks involved. The seller's main risk is if the stock increases fairly quickly, the seller still has to sell at the agreed-upon strike price.

The buyer's main risk is the stock not increasing in value and thereby losing money by having paid the premium.

This might seem complicated and time-intensive, but it's fairly quick and easy to setup. You can write call options in less than a minute.

The final and my most favorite way to make money with stocks (I saved the best for last), is by receiving dividends from the stocks you own. The main focus of this book is evaluating dividend-paying stocks. There is a reason why I listed certain companies, like Coke, Proctor and Gamble and Philip Morris, that the billionaires invest in, in the introduction. First, because these are high-quality companies that investors also need to think about investing in. Secondly, these are companies that pay out a dividend quarterly.

What's a dividend?

A **dividend** is cold hard cash that a company pays to its shareholders frequently. Most US dividend-paying companies dish out dividends 4 times a year (every quarter). The only dividend-paying stocks I look for are stocks that increase their dividends faster than inflation, each year. This keeps my money growing faster than inflation. This is extremely important; **I want to have my money grow faster than inflation!!**

Inflation is the rise in prices of goods and services over time. This means your money will buy fewer goods or services because it decreased in value.

For example, if inflation is 3%, a box of candy that costs $1 today will cost $1.03 next year.

Most companies that pay out a dividend are usually blue-chip companies. These are more stable, well-established companies with shares outstanding in the billions. Because they are more well-established and have been in business for many years, they can pay a **stable dividend** to their shareholders.

In times of economic turmoil, blue-chip stocks also get hit, but they are usually able to bounce back as investors tend to gravitate towards them for their stability.

According to folklore, the first dividend was paid out by the VOC. The VOC was a company that traveled to Asia to "trade" commodities with other cultures.

The ships that were needed to travel to Asia took quite a beating from tough winds, storms, and other natural disasters.

Not only did the Dutch need more ships, because the market was booming, they also wanted to ensure their ships from these natural disasters. They decided to sell shares in the company to their citizens and in return for buying these shares, they would also receive a dividend.

Why do companies pay out dividends?
Most companies pay out a dividend to their shareholders as a repayment for the money that the shareholders put in the company, by buying the initial shares. You can also see it as a reward to you as a shareholder who bought stock in the company.

You invest and believe in the company and in return, the company gives you a piece of the profit. But don't forget that the company used your money and other shareholders' capital to invest back into the business to hopefully improve the overall value of the business.

Also, paying out dividends increases shareholder's loyalty to the company.

When a public company or one that is about to go public needs to raise a large amount of cash, to expand their business, pay down debt, buy equipment, etc., it can do a couple of things:

- Loan money from banks
- Sell more of its goods or services
- Issue shares or go public
- Use its equity
- Issue a bond

If the company loans money from the bank, it has to pay the bank back with interest and to sell more goods or services, the company needs fresh new capital to expand whereby it can sell more. So a company might rather decide to issue shares.

The benefit of this is that the company decides how many shares it wants to issue to the public. The capital generated from selling these shares on the stock market is then invested back into the business to increase the value of the business. Best of all, the company does not owe the bank any money, because it did not take out a loan.

A company only makes money from its shares when it goes public (**IPO**). Going public means a private company sells its shares to stockholders on the stock market. Once these shares are sold, they are in the hands of shareholders and they decide to buy or sell amongst themselves.

You can kind of look at it like a video game company that produces a new game, but only creates 100,000 copies. They end up selling out all the copies of this new game so the video game company has made its money.

The buyers of these copies are now the owners. They can decide to keep the game or sell it to other potential customers for a suitable price.

When a company goes public, the amount it sells it shares for and the amounts of shares it will sell are the two most important factors to think about. You don't want to sell your shares too cheap, because that is money that the company will use to improve its core business.

So, if the company does not make any more money from shares it sold on the stock market, why does it care about the stock price?

One reason is that management themselves own shares of the company. They usually receive a **compensation package** that also includes shares in the company. It is, therefore, in their best interest to run the company successfully which should increase the share price of the stock.

Another reason is that companies frequently buy their stocks back, leaving fewer shares outstanding on the stock market.

Often a company reissues shares it bought back if it needs to raise some capital. Issuing shares dilutes your ownership. If a company has 100,000 shares outstanding and you own 10,000, you own 10% of the company. If the company ends up reissuing 50,000 more shares, the total amount of shares outstanding is now 150,000. You still own 10,000, but instead of 10% ownership, you now own 6.7% (10,000/150,000) of the company.

However, as long as a company buys back more shares than it reissues, this should not be a big concern.

Making money is the main reason that investors or shareholders buy stocks. Out of the four ways explained to make money, most people like buying low and selling high, because it's the easiest to understand. But there is a community of investors, called value investors, who would rather buy shares in high-quality companies at a discount and hold them for a long period while receiving growing dividends along the way.

Chapter Two: Secret to Financial Independence

The plan for financial freedom

The plan is to buy companies that pay out dividends that grow faster than **inflation**. The dividends received are reinvested or used to buy other companies' stock. This puts an investor's dividend income growth on the fast track, because not only is there constant access to fresh investment capital through automatic transfers, the investor also uses the dividends received to snowball and compound wealth.

Once an investor builds up his or her dividend income to match or exceed the income generated from their career, they will finally be financially free. Because now they could just live off the income generated from dividends, without having to sell the underlying assets, which are the investments.

Once this point is reached, investors also won't have to worry about inflation as their dividend income will keep up and even exceed inflation. They also have an added benefit that these dividend-paying blue-chip companies are more stable and will increase in value along the way.

To receive a dividend you first need to buy a share in a company that pays out a dividend. We'll look into finding these companies and deciding which one is right for a healthy portfolio.

The biggest benefits of dividends are that they are more reliable than capital gains, which are the gains your investment make in the stock market, and by doing a little bit of research you should be able to create a portfolio of high-quality dividend-paying stocks.

Consistency from dividends is important, because this allows investors to plan their potential income far into the future. There are many companies that consistently raise their dividends.

For example, a company like Coca Cola has paid out an increasing dividend for the last 50 years and in the last 10 years, they've been able to increase their dividend at an average rate of about 8.96% (8.45% in the last 5 years).

Table 2.1 Coca Cola Company Dividend Growth Rate

Coca-Cola	2010	2011	2012	2013	2014	2015
Dividend	$0.88	$0.94	$1.02	$1.12	$1.22	$1.32
Dividend growth rate		6.82%	8.51%%	9.80%	8.93%	8.20%

Now you might be thinking, "big deal, I buy a couple of shares and I'll receive a little bit in dividend income, it's not worth it."

The best way to grow income fast with dividends is to constantly buy stocks in blue-chip companies that pay out dividends and then reinvest these dividends that you received to buy more dividend-paying stocks or reinvest them in the same companies.

This will result in a snowball effect, whereby you start small and along the way your snowball keeps growing up to a point where you don't have to push it anymore since it's able to roll on its own. Also called the compound effect, where you are making money on your money.

Dividend income is **realized income**, so once received, the recipient is free to do with it what he or she wants. Most people are familiar with a 401k because the company that they work with might offer their employees one, with a company match.

When you invest in a 401k the money that you make or lose is **unrealized income**, because your money is still in the market.

If the value of your 401k increases, we call it a **capital gain**, because your money (capital) has gained in value. Vice versa, a loss is called a capital loss. As long as you keep your capital in the stock market it has a chance to increase or decrease in value.

Your unrealized gains or losses only become realized once you sell your investments.

So to summarize, dividends are realized income that a company pays to its shareholders. Once received, the shareholder decides what he or she wants to do with that dividend. They can reinvest it, buy other investments, pay their bills, buy food, go shopping, etc.

Now while looking at the graph earlier, keep in mind that I left out inflation and taxes. The average inflation rate is around 3.2%-3.5%, so if an investor can buy companies that pay a dividend that increases faster than inflation (minimum of 4%), they will be able to keep their spending power.

Right now dividends are taxed depending on the investor's income and their investment account.

Getting paid dividends

The directors of a company decide what the dividend payment should be and when it should be paid out to shareholders. The day of the announcement is also called the **declaration date**. Let's look at an example of Coca Cola's declared dividends for the last 2 years:

Table 2.2 Coca Cola Company Dividend Dates

Cash Amount	Declaration Date	Ex/Eff-Dividend Date	Record Date	Payment Date	Frequency
$0.33	10/15/2015	11/27/2015	12/1/2015	12/15/2015	Quarter
$0.33	7/16/2015	9/11/2015	9/15/2015	10/1/2015	Quarter
$0.33	4/30/2015	6/11/2015	6/15/2015	7/1/2015	Quarter
$0.33	2/19/2015	3/12/2015	3/16/2015	4/1/2015	Quarter
$0.31	10/16/2014	11/26/2014	12/1/2014	12/15/2014	Quarter
$0.31	7/15/2014	9/11/2014	9/15/2014	10/1/2014	Quarter
$0.31	4/24/2014	6/12/2014	6/16/2014	7/1/2014	Quarter
$0.31	2/20/2014	3/12/2014	3/14/2014	4/1/2014	Quarter

Cash amount is the amount of dividend you will receive for one stock. So if you own 10 you want to multiply the cash amount by 10. The **declaration date** as stated above is the date that the directors announce when the next payment will be, the ex-dividend date and the amount of that payment.

The **ex/eff-dividend date** is the date by which you need to own the stock to receive the upcoming dividend payment.

The **record date** is the cut-off date a company uses to determine which shareholders will receive the dividend.

Payment date is self-explanatory and **frequency** is how frequent the dividend is paid out by the company. Most US companies pay out a dividend quarterly, but some companies pay out monthly dividends.

The quickest way to learn the different dates:

We'll tell you how much we'll pay you (declaration)

You need to own the actual shares to receive a dividend (ex-eff)

We'll check to see if you own the shares (record)

We'll pay you (payment)

The dividend neglect

So how come dividends aren't more popular? Because the majority of investors don't care about dividends, they want to **make money fast** through capital gains.

The story of the tortoise and the hare is a great example of how people operate in the stock market. If you don't know the story, you can find the cartoon on Youtube.com.

The tortoise (dividend) is the one that everyone laughs at and neglects, but the hare (capital gains) attracts all the attention because he is flashy and exciting. Throughout history the hare has made millionaires out of paupers, but even more important, the hare has made people go broke even faster.

Throughout that time the tortoise has been steadily chugging along, throughout the great depression of 1929, the dotcom crash of 2000, and the recent recession of 2008.

Many companies like Johnson & Johnson, Proctor & Gamble, Dover, and Unilever still paid an increasing dividend throughout the recent recession and it is these same boring dividend-paying companies that people flock to when economic turmoil is upon us.

Now many companies cut or slashed their dividends in 2008, but even many of these companies bounced back fairly quickly and continued paying dividends.

People love their capital gains and that's what fuels the investment companies. They know that people want to see their money grow fast, that's why you see companies advertising their mutual funds with a 1-year return of 21%, 5-year return of 20% and a ten-year return of 11%.

Then when the market crashes, everybody panics and starts selling at a huge loss.

Using the Coca Cola returns from earlier as an example, the initial returns are nothing to brag about, 3.3% the first year ($331.9/$10,000), 3.72% the second year, and 4.2% the third year.

The average investor would laugh at those returns and go with a mutual fund, ETF, or index fund that generates a higher return, but the tortoise keeps chugging along and at year 34 has a return or otherwise known as yield on cost of **13519.32%.**

Your dividend income future

Now to speed up the process of building a stable dividend income portfolio, because no one wants to wait 34 years before they can enjoy the fruits of their labor, investors should start as early as possible. This will allow investors to have a longer time frame for their dividends to grow.

Secondly, investors should invest regularly and not just once like in the example I showed you. Also, investors need to make sure to use the dividend income they receive to buy stock in other dividend companies or reinvest the dividend in the same company.

It's ok for investors to start with a small amount and once they get more comfortable and see those dividends rolling in constantly, they can increase the amount of money they use for investing.

They will then be able to track their dividend income and growth since this is far more stable than capital gains. For example, if an investor has a goal of receiving $100,000 in dividend income, they'll be able to calculate how much they need to invest regularly, what their dividend growth rate must be, and how many years it will take for them to hit this goal.

Also, if working at a job is not providing enough money to invest, then additional avenues need to be explored for making extra money.

Work a second job, starting a side business, getting into rental income properties or creating and selling products are good places to start. Whatever the side hustle is, it has to be **legal**.

So, if investors plan on retiring within 20, 15, 10, or even 5 years with a dividend income strategy, it behooves them to be **more diligent** with investing and reinvesting their dividends to create wealth faster.

How come not all companies pay out dividends?

Every single business in existence goes through the business life cycle. There are many stages in a business life cycle; we will look at 4 different stages.

A business always starts as an idea and moves through different stages. One of the first stages is the start-up phase. These are fairly new companies that might get funding from a venture capitalist or angel investors. You will often hear on the news or the internet about high-tech companies in the start-up phase.

Once the business gains some momentum by finding a customer base and fine-tuning its products or services, it will switch over to the growth phase.

Now a company can either be profitable in the growth stage or the owners might have a plan to get it into the profit zone.

In the growth phase, a company might also decide to initiate an IPO, which means an initial public offering. This is when the company makes its shares available on the stock market. These companies are focused on growing, so any money that they receive or generate is reinvested back into the company. For example, companies like Google, Twitter, and Tesla.

In the maturity phase, a company has been able to penetrate the market, find its foothold, and finally become stable. Think about companies like Walmart or Unilever. These companies don't take too many risks, because they are established. It is at the maturity stage that most companies start paying out dividends.

Once the products or services from a company fall out of favor with its customers, the company will shift into the decline phase and phase out. Think of products like cassette tapes, Polaroid pictures, and the Walkman.

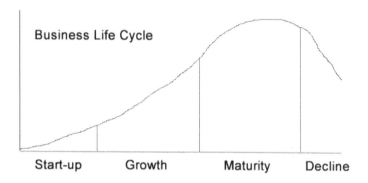

Figure 2.1 Basic Business Cycle

Where do dividends come from?

Companies pay out dividends from the net income they generate. The net income is the bottom line earnings of the company. So this is the profit or loss a company ends up with after all their expenses, employee salaries, taxes, etc. are paid.

A company can do a couple of things with their earnings:

- Invest it in new projects
- Buy or fix equipment, buildings
- Buyback shares outstanding
- Pay down debt
- Pay out dividends to shareholders

Most companies that pay out dividends are sitting on piles of cash that they don't have to reinvest back in the business. Most of these companies can also pay down their long term debt within a couple of years. It is best for these companies to either buy back their shares or pay their shareholders a dividend who can then take this money and invest it in other companies or do with it whatever they want. Most companies do a combination of these different things with their earnings.

The stock market

SuperDot, market makers, bid/ask spread, level 2 quotes, intraday trading, Fibonacci and who could ever forget the dead cat bounce. Oh yes, the stock market can get somewhat complicated, but let's try to keep it simple.

The stock market facilitates the buying and selling of securities such as stocks, currencies, commodities, and futures.

The trading of stocks happens on **stock exchanges**. These can be on a physical trading floor or a virtual one. If you've ever seen the movie Trading Places, you've seen what a trading floor used to look like.

People are yelling and screaming, making hand gestures, and pieces of paper are flying everywhere. Nowadays, it's less noisy, because brokers can initiate trades on their handheld gadgets. So there is no need to yell and holler sell and buy prices.

The most prominent stock exchanges in the US are the New York Stock Exchange and the NASDAQ. It's on these two stock exchanges that you can trade most of the companies in the US. Also, the NASDAQ is virtual, so there is no trading floor.

Many developed nations have their own stock exchanges. The United Kingdom has the London Stock Exchange, Canada has the Toronto Stock Exchange and the Netherlands has the AEX, and so on.

On what stock exchange a company trades depends mostly on its market cap. The market capitalization of a company is calculated by taking the amount of shares outstanding times the share price. The market cap is the total value of a company on the stock market.

So if a company is trading at $20 and has 1 billion shares outstanding, the market cap of this company would be $20,000,000,000. Big, well-known companies like Walmart and McDonalds have a market cap in the billions.

The most used classifications are:

- Large-cap: $10 billion or more market cap
- Mid-cap: between $2 billion and $10 billion
- Small-cap: less than $2 billion

You might also hear about nano-cap and micro-cap, but the most used market cap classifications are the three mentioned earlier.

Smaller cap companies are listed on the OTC stock exchange and pink sheets. These smaller companies could be micro-cap stocks, nano-cap, or even penny stocks.

Stocks on these stock exchanges are unregulated so you should be extra careful when investing in these types of stocks.

Don't get scammed and slammed

Many people get scammed by being promised easy riches. What usually happens is a salesman reaches out to you by phone, internet, or even in person. He will give you a sales pitch about a shady company or investment and you fall for the pitch because all you can see are dollar signs.

So you end up owning shares in this company and everything seems to be going good in the beginning, then all of a sudden the stock price tanks and you just lost your shirt.

You just experienced a **pump and dump**. This is how it works: a company is trading on the OTCBB stock exchange. Now, this company might be a real company or a fake one that doesn't even have employees.

This company's shares are trading at a low price, so a con man buys a lot of shares for cheap in this company. They then start advertising this company and the price of the stock starts to increase. Once it has increased up to a certain point, the scammer sells all his shares at this high price and makes a killing.

The price of the stock immediately drops and people start panicking and sell their shares at a huge loss. So the conman pumped up the price of the shares by getting many investors to purchase these shares in the hope of making money. Then he sells all his shares which sparks the fast decline of the price of the stock, which would be the dump.

A conman, in this case, might be a person, a group of people, or even legitimate banks and investment companies.

However, there are day traders, investors who buy and sell stocks within a day, that can see a pump and dump coming from a mile away and can make a killing by playing the market. Average investors should stay far away from this technique.

Where to buy stocks?

Investors like you and I don't have the time to go to New York and start selling and buying shares on the New York Stock Exchange (NYSE) trading floor.

This is where a **broker** comes in to play. A broker is a firm that handles the buying and selling of securities on your behalf, at a commission.

There are **full-service brokers** and **discount brokers**. Full-service brokers give you investment advice and charge a higher commission for selling or buying equity.

The internet has propelled the discount broker. These brokers have cut the cost of commissions for their investors and let them do all the leg work for deciding which companies to invest in. I **only** use discount brokers for buying dividend-paying stocks.

In the ancient days, you would open your newspaper and read about stock quotes, you would then visit or call your broker and let him know that you wanted to buy or sell stocks. He would send a message out to the marketplace, by placing a phone call. A representative of your brokerage firm would pick up and write on a piece of paper your order. He would walk over to the trading floor and give your order to the floor broker who would then try to negotiate a good price for you.

The floor consists of both buyers and sellers, so when the negotiation takes place, it involves yelling out buy or sell orders and making hand gestures to let buyers or sellers know that they want to buy on behalf of their client, what the price will be and how many securities.

Once the order is complete, your broker will get a confirmation phone call. He will then tell you that your order was executed successfully or call you at home and leave you a message. For using the services of your broker you paid a commission, which was more than $100 for a trade.

Nowadays, you can still go to your broker's office or call them to place an order. But with the advancement that the internet has brought us, you can execute orders yourself online through discount brokers. Commission cost has come down considerably, with average commissions between $5-$10.

Stock chart

You can track the performance of every stock online. One website that I like to use is **Google Finance**.

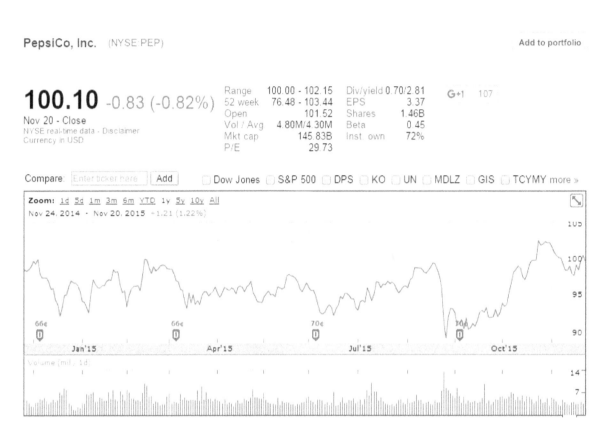

Figure 3.1 PepsiCo Stock Chart Starting From January 2015. Source: Google Finance

If you look at the image above you'll notice we are looking at the Pepsi stock. Every stock on a stock exchange has a **ticker symbol**. PepsiCo ticker is **PEP**.

You can see the price movement of the stock, in this case by month, and if you hover over the chart, you will see additional information about the stock at a specific period. On the right side, you see numbers that represent a dollar amount, so 100 is $100 and 95 is $95, etc. You can, therefore, follow the price of the stock at a specific date.

The volume chart below is the number of trades placed for the stock.

The letter D on the chart is the ex/eff dividend date and above that is the dividend amount.

The stock chart moves from left to right, many investors are glued to stock charts and decide to buy and sell depending on where they think the price will move to.

You can see that the stock closed at $100.10 on November 20th. Next to the price of the stock, you see the **range** of the day; this is the range the stock was trading for the day.

The **52-week** is the range the stock was trading at for the last 52 weeks. **Open** is what price the stock started trading for the day. **The average volume** is the amount of buying and selling of shares. **Market cap** is the price of the stock times the number of shares outstanding, which also represents the total value of the company on the stock market.

We will go into more debt about the P/E, dividend yield, and EPS.

Shares represent the number of shares outstanding on the stock market. Investors trade these shares with each other.

Beta is the historical volatility of the stock compared to the market. A higher beta means the stock is more volatile in terms of its price movement. Higher beta stocks are considered higher risk.

Institutional ownership shows you the percentage of shares outstanding in the hands of investment banks, mutual funds, pension funds, retirement accounts, and more.

There is, of course, a lot more that can be said about stock charts, it is best to start familiarizing yourself with it by checking it out frequently.

S&P 500

You might hear about the **S&P 500** in the news a lot. The S&P 500 tracks 500 large-cap US companies stocks. These stocks represent the overall economy. So you might hear on the news that the S&P 500 increased by 200 **points** (one point is one dollar). That means that all the 500 companies the S&P tracks on average increased.

Now if the S&P 500 has been losing points daily, it might mean that the stock market is pessimistic about the economy and it's trending downwards.

Some of the companies that the S&P 500 tracks are: Exxon Mobil, Apple, Microsoft, Proctor and Gamble, General Electric. These companies also hold a considerable amount of weight in the S&P 500.

There are other indexes like the Dow Jones, which tracks 30 large-cap companies. You also have the S&P Small Cap 600 and the S&P midcap 400, the Russell 2000 index and the list goes on. An index is used to gauge the performance of its underlying companies.

2-1 split

Every once in awhile a company might decide to do a 2 for 1 stock split. This means that a company is dividing the number of stocks they have outstanding. If a company's stock price was $110 and it had $1 million shares outstanding after a 2-1 split the stock price would be $55 and there are now $2 million shares.

Companies do this when their stock price becomes too high. This might scare investors in purchasing such a high stock price. After a 2-1 split, the share of the company looks more affordable. Another reason is for **liquidity**, which means the ease of selling and buying of the stock.

If there are more shares on the market at a cheaper price, it makes the stock more liquid.

If you are an investor who owns the stock, a 2-1 split will give you double the number of shares. So if you had 30 stocks, a 2-1 will give you 30 extra for a total of 60 stocks. The price of the stock and your dividends are halved, but totaling up your shares will give you the same dividend amount and share amount you had before the 2-1 split.

Are you scared of the market?

Many people are too afraid to invest in the market, because they have been burned, or they know someone who has been burned. Let's look at some of the most memorable stock market crashes.

The stock market crash of 1929

The crash of 1929 which led to the great depression has been the worst in history. Before the crash, the economy was booming, everyday citizens were making money, and they were looking at other avenues to grow their wealth.

Many investors were familiar with government bonds that the government issued to fund the war. People started speculating in the stock market and buying many stocks on margin. This allowed investors to borrow money to buy stocks.

So you could put down a certain percentage, let's say 30% to buy stocks and your broker would loan you the other 70%. There was no rule set up to limit the amount you could borrow on margin.

To make matters even worse, many brokers were advising their clients to buy on margin, since everyone was doing it and it was a quick way to make money fast.

One problem with **buying on margin**, besides it being high risk, is that if the stocks you buy fall below a certain threshold your broker will call in the margin. This means that you will have to pay all the money that you loaned back to your broker.

When the market crashed, all the people that bought their stocks on margin not only lost the money that they invested in the market, they also lost the money they borrowed from the broker. In those days, many people put their whole retirement savings in the market.

Since the value of the securities (stocks) fell below a certain threshold, the brokers started calling in the margins. This left people broke and bankrupt.

Buying on margin was of course not the only element that led to the Great Depression, but it did play a huge part. You can still buy securities on margin, but there are limits placed on how much you can borrow.

In the early 1920s the stock market was only accessed by a small group of people, also known as **Wall Street**. These were the big financial institutions, such as banks, but also rich and wealthy individuals of that time. By introducing **Main Street** to the stock market, which are retail investors like you and me, a new injection of capital flooded the stock market.

Not everyone lost money in those days, though. Many insiders, big banks, and brokers started buying stocks at a cheap price, pumping up the stock and when retail investors jumped in to buy these stocks, the big banks dumped their shares back on the market, making millions in the process and leaving Main Street with these stocks that ended up crashing. They used the old pump and dump method.

The market works on greed and fear, when a stock is climbing higher, many people start taking notice and jump on board and try to ride this seemingly endless increase in stock price.

The reverse also holds true, people's fears kick in when a stock that they own drops in value. Once an increasingly large number of investors start selling, everybody jumps on board and starts selling also, because they are afraid they will lose everything.

Because of the great depression, President Roosevelt set up the **Security and Exchange Commission**. The SEC regulates the securities market. It enforces the law and has to make sure it is scrupulous in protecting investors.

Dotcom crash

The Dotcom crash took place at the beginning of this millennium and lasted for a few years. Many people called the dotcom era the new economy. This was supposed to be an age where the sky was the limit because everything happened in cyberspace. There were no physical limitations; the only limit was in your mind. A 12-year-old kid could set up a website and get traffic flowing to it and without making any money he could sell the same site for millions, based on the potential of the site. Stories of young people becoming millionaires overnight were not uncommon.

Venture capitalists started flooding the market with cash, buying websites that never made any money. They then turned these private internet companies public through an **IPO** (initial public offering), which made it possible for retail investors to buy stock in these websites.

People started getting greedy and started buying stocks in internet companies like no tomorrow. They neglected companies like Emerson Electric, Dover, and Proctor & Gamble, because those companies were old and boring. Why invest in companies that pay a dividend but see a slower increase in their stock price when you can buy an internet stock that has the chance of increasing over 40% in value in a couple of days?

Most of these internet companies never made any money, but people started valuing these companies on how many clicks they got or how many visitors went to the site daily. Everybody was buying these stocks based on the potential of these companies, even highly reputable investment banks and brokers were advising their clients to ditch other safer stocks and buy internet stocks instead.

The greed of investors shot up many stocks into the stratosphere and a bubble started forming. This bubble burst in 2000 and many people lost more than they could stomach.

Everybody lost money, right? Not exactly, the same bankers and venture capitalist who owned many of these internet companies when they were private, were able to sell their shares in these companies, after they went public with their IPO, and made millions in the process by selling these overvalued shares to retail investors.

The money they made was then used to play the same game over and over again, buying other internet companies and going through with the IPO. They were the first to own the overvalued shares at a cheap price and after the price of the stock was pumped up high enough, they dumped their stocks on the market by selling them.

The old pump and dump never fails, always catching greedy retail investors and eventually leaving them broke.

The Great Recession

The Great Recession was kicked into high gear, by the boom and bust of the housing market. Investors looking to invest their money and receive a greater return on their investment started speculating in the housing market. Eventually, mortgage lenders loaned money to high-risk citizens who ended up defaulting on their mortgage payments. The lender then ends up getting the house. As more people started defaulting, the lender ended up with an increased amount of houses that they did not receive any mortgage payments on.

Prices on homes dropped all over the country, because of the large number of vacant houses. This sharp decline in housing prices left the homeowners that were still paying their mortgage wondering why they were paying off a mortgage of let's say $200,000, while the house now is only worth $70,000.

This housing crisis did not only affect rich investors because other institutions like commercial banks and lenders also had skin in the game. What happened was similar to a domino effect. Everything started falling down.

And since many financial institutions worldwide also had their hands in the cookie jar, their nations felt this collapse, also.

But here is the interesting part. If we take a look at the stock chart for Pepsi, you can see that the crash started in the middle of 2008. The price of PepsiCo stock went as high as $78.46 at the end of 2007 and dropped as low as $47.10 in 2009. The stock dropped 39.96%. But look at the dividends that Pepsi paid out. Before, during and after this whole debacle, Pepsi never stopped paying and increasing its dividend.

Figure 3.1 PepsiCo Stock Chart Starting From 2007. Source: Google Finance

Opening a brokerage account

To start buying stocks in different companies, you need to have a **brokerage account**. Setting up a brokerage account is easy and you can set one up online.

Some of the most well-known brokerage accounts at the moment are:

- Ally
- Etrade
- Capital One Investing
- TD Ameritrade

A quick google search and you can find many more. It's always best to shop around and compare features from all these different brokerage accounts.

While comparing, here is what you should look for:

- Commission rates (cost per trade)
- Customer service ratings
- Minimum deposit
- Different tools available
- No cost dividend reinvestment plan (DRP)

I recommend checking out Tradeking.com. You can have your account up and running in no time, they also have pretty good research tools.

Opening an account is free, they allow DRPs, and their commission rate at the moment is only $4.95.

The dividend reinvestment plan (DRP) allows you to reinvest the dividends that you receive. You can start a DRP with just one share; the dividend that you receive will allow you to buy a portion of a share, commission-free. So, if you received a $1 dividend and the stock that it will be reinvested in is trading for $50, you will purchase 2% of the share ($1/$50).

When you log into your brokerage account you will see how much funds you have in your account available to trade. You can add more money or transfer money out of your account from the cash balance depending on which account type you own.

Each brokerage account has a different interface, but most of them will have the basic features, such as buying and selling stocks, your account balance, security research tools, customer service, order status, and history.

The best way to get comfortable with the interface will be to just go in, start clicking around and learn how the system works. You can also reach out to customer service and every account usually has a help section you can browse through.

Brokerage account type

Whenever you setup your account, you will also select your account type. See below for a list of the most prominent accounts:

- Traditional individual brokerage account
- IRA/Roth IRA (individual retirement account)
- SEP
- 401k/403(b)
- 529 Plans
- Education savings account
- Qualified plans
- Health savings account
- MyRA (My retirement account)

Each account has its nuances, for example, a traditional account allows you to buy any type of equity on the market. There are no limits on how much money you can deposit in this account. You will, however, have to pay taxes on dividends and capital gains if you sell your shares because this is a **taxable account**.

The **401K** retirement account is what most people are familiar with because most companies now allow their employees to enroll in one. A 401k is an employer-sponsored retirement plan. Most often there is also a company match to entice employees to invest in their 401k. The 401k is an example of a **tax-deferred account**.

The **IRA** and **Roth IRA** are both popular accounts that you can open if your employer does not offer a 401k. You can also open these accounts even if you already have a 401k.

With an IRA you end up paying taxes once you withdraw money out of your account at retirement age. With a Roth IRA, on the other hand, you pay taxes on your income now and you can withdraw money tax-free when you are retired. The age at which you can start withdrawing is 59.5. This, however, might change in the future.

With the 401k and the IRA/Roth IRA accounts, there are certain penalties you should pay attention to if you plan on withdrawing your money early. You will be hit with a 10% early withdrawal penalty. There are exceptions, however, qualified first-time home-buyers can withdraw up to $10k penalty-free and your Roth IRA contributions can be withdrawn tax-free. Just the contributions, though, not the capital gains, dividends or money you received from options.

If you work at a company that offers a 401k with a company match, you should take advantage of that, because the company match is free money given to you.

If you're just starting out buying stocks in individual companies, I suggest you open a Roth IRA account. You won't have to pay taxes on **qualified** dividends that you receive and you can reinvest these dividends to let your money grow.

I can go on forever about the advantages and disadvantages of all these accounts, but make sure you talk to a professional advisor about your options and choices. To keep it simple I would do this:

If I worked at a company that offers a 401k, I would be sure to enroll in one especially if my company pays a match. Next, I would open a Roth IRA account with any of the previously listed brokerage firms, I recommend Tradeking.com, to start trading. Last, if I am comfortable buying and selling stocks, I would also open a traditional brokerage account.

I would then have immediate access to the dividends I received, but I will have to pay taxes on my dividend income, depending on the state I live in and my income.

Buying a stock

Buying or selling stocks online is even easier than shopping online. You navigate to the trading section of your brokerage account. You specify if you want to buy or sell a stock, enter the number of shares you want to buy, enter the ticker symbol (you will get a pop up that shows you what the current price of the stock is on the market), enter the order type, and the duration.

Hit review or preview order, and submit your order. Depending on the order type that you choose, the order might complete immediately. Once the order is complete you will see the stock in your portfolio after about 3 business days. That's it!

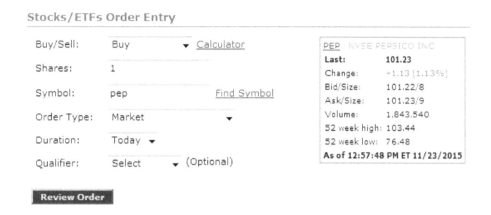

Figure 4.1 Buying One Share in a Scottrade Account

Whenever you are buying stocks online, you will notice a couple of different order types. The market, limit, stop, stop limit, and trailing stop order.

A **market order** is an order that fires immediately, so once you place an order for 1 share of Pepsi, you will receive 1 stock at the market price at that moment. The market does not stay still, so looking at the image the $101.23 for a Pepsi stock could be a different price just once second later. This is for both buying and selling of stock.

A **limit order** allows you to buy or sell stock at a certain price. Let's say I wanted to pay $100 for the Pepsi stock above, I could put a limit order for $100. This order will only execute once the price of the Pepsi stock drops down to $100 or beyond. This is my **favorite** order type when placing orders.

With a **stop order**, you place a stop price to buy or sell stock. If I put a stop order for $101, the order will wait until the price drops down to $101 and it will then turn into a market order and execute.

Many investors use this stop order to prevent them from taking further losses. If you know you bought a stock at a certain price and would sell at another price, you could use a stop order. If an investor bought the Pepsi stock for $101 and would want to sell it if it dropped to $80, the investor could use a stop order.

A **stop limit order** is a combination of the stop and a limit order. The stop price will convert this order into a buy or sell order and the limit price will be the price at which the order will execute.

A **trailing stop** is mostly used by investors who want to sell their stock and still enjoy a quick profit from the sale. With a trailing stop, you specify a percentage or points at which you would want to sell under the market price.

If you bought stock at $50 and you put a sell trailing stop at 10% if the price of the stock falls down to $45 the stock would sell because it hit that 10% you specified. Now, if the stock moved up to $55 the trailing stop at 10% would trail the stock also and would now only sell if the stock dropped to $49.50 because 10% of $55 is $5.50. So the trailing stop would execute at $55-$5.50 = $49.50.

Selling a stock

Whenever you sell your stocks you need to know what the accompanying tax burden will be. If you even have to pay taxes will first depend on what type of brokerage account you are using. You are either using a **tax-deferred** or a **taxable account**.

With a taxable account, you will have to pay taxes on the sale of stocks and the dividends you received. With a tax-deferred account, however, these taxes are deferred until a later date, paid upfront, or until a particular date.

If you are using a taxable account, you will have to pay a capital gains tax, which is the profits you received from the rise of the stocks after you purchased it, if you held the stocks longer than a year.

If you held them less than a year and sold them, you will have to pay your ordinary income tax rate. If you had a capital loss you can deduct the loss up to a certain amount from your tax bill.

The selling of stocks itself is really easy. All the different buy order types apply to the sell orders, but there is an additional sell order called **Sell Short**, which we have explained in Chapter One.

Commission

Whenever you buy or sell stocks you have to pay your brokerage firm a **commission fee**. The commission fee is usually between $5 to $10 at online discount brokers.

There is no set rule on this, but whenever I buy stocks, I make sure that the commission is **1% or less** of the total order. If my commission is $4.95, I try to buy around $500 worth of stocks or more.

The reason for this is you would otherwise pay too much in commission. If you bought 3 shares at $20 apiece and your commission fee is $4.95. Your total order would be $64.95. Your commission would be 7.6% ($4.95/$64.95) of your total order, which is too high a price to pay.

Chapter Five: Your Money Is Not Safe!

Best place to save your money

Is the best place to park your money in the stock market or not? What other vehicles can you use park to your money?

Under the mattress

Just saving cash and keeping it on hand year after year is not the smartest thing to do. Besides the immediate threat of someone breaking in and stealing your money or your house burning down, you also have to think about inflation and how it will impact your spending power in the future.

Savings Account

Back in 2006-07, you could get a savings account with a 5-6% interest rate. Nowadays, you'll be lucky if you can get one above 1%. Even though money in a savings account seems safe, it's losing its purchasing power. If inflation on average is 3.5% per year, which means goods and services will get more expensive next year, then your dollar today is only worth 96.5 cents next year.

Most people keep their money in a savings account for fear of losing it if they invested it. But throughout the years your money is worthless. This also goes for CDs, since their interest rates have declined, also.

Mutual funds

A mutual fund is a fund where a large group of investors' money is pooled together and then used to invest in different securities such as stocks and bonds.

If you buy shares in a mutual fund you own a small percentage of these different securities, which makes for a diversified portfolio.

As you know by now, stocks are considered the riskiest investments. To limit that risk a financial professional, who manages a mutual fund, tries to spread the risk over a large number of securities.

The problem with mutual funds is that there are many fees associated with them, such as management fees, administrative fees, reinvestment fees, front-end load, back-end load, and more.

The fee that I always look at is the expense ratio, which is the percentage that your financial institution charges yearly. These expense ratios can range from under 0.5% to above 1%.

If you had an investment capital of $100,000 in this mutual fund, with a 0.5% expense ratio you would pay $500 in expenses for that year. If after a few years your investment grew to $200,000, you would now pay $1,000 at a .5% expense ratio.

That is a high price to pay because you could have taken that $1,000 and invested it yourself. Keep in mind that when you buy stocks yourself, the only cost you have to pay is the **commission fee** when you buy or sell securities.

Another problem with mutual funds is that you lose your voting rights. The institution or financial professional that owns the mutual fund has all the voting rights.

401K

Most companies now offer their employees the option to contribute percentage or fixed dollar amount to their 401k.

I like the 401k, but whenever you sign up for one at work, your options on what you can invest in are limited to what investment plans the company offers.

Popular 401k funds right now are the **target-date retirement funds**. These usually have a year at the end, like Vanguard Target Retirement 2055. The year represents the year of retirement, which means that the fund might start out with having 70-80% of the portfolio in stocks, but the closer it gets to your retirement date of 2055, it's going to gradually rebalance the portfolio to increase safer investments like bonds and decrease the allocation of riskier investments like stocks.

Same as with the mutual funds, there are expenses that you need to pay attention to and you don't have voting rights.

Index funds and ETFs

It seems like everybody is ranting and raving about index funds and ETFs. There are plenty of studies online that show that most financial planners cannot consistently beat the market.

So, you have an index like the S&P 500 which represents the 500 biggest companies of the US. A financial planner's job might be to beat the S&P 500 and when looking at a 10-year frame, most financial planners underperform the market.

So here you are, paying all these expenses to a financial institution and on average they cannot even beat the market.

This is where index funds come in. An index fund invests in the same companies as the index it tracks and holds the same weight percentage of these securities. It's basically a mirror of the index it tracks.

A very popular one is the VFINX, it has a low expense ratio of .17%. Expenses are so low on index funds because they are managed by computers. Minimal human involvement is necessary compared to mutual funds and target-date retirement funds.

Even though there are many different index funds and ETF investments, my first concern is that they invest in companies that I would not invest in.

If you just look at the top companies by weight that are in the S&P 500, you will see a lot of tech companies that don't pay a dividend and large banks. The only banks I invest in are local banks that keep their financial books easy to analyze.

The problem with bigger banks is that they complicate their business practices on purpose. It then gets up to a point where no one is held accountable if something goes wrong. Because of the complicated nature of bigger banks, it's hard to hold someone accountable.

With index funds, your wealth only increases when your shares increase in value (stock moves up in price), there are only 3 directions a stock can move: up, down, or sideways.

Figure 5.1 Growth of $10,000 in The Stock Market. Source: Morningstar.com

If you had $10k invested in an index fund at the end of November 2005 (1), your money would grow to $12,630 at its peak in 2007 (2), but let's look at 2009. Your invested $10k is worth only $6,192.86 at its lowest point (3) on February 28, 2009, because the stock market crashed and it took until March 2010 to reach and pass the $10,000 mark (4).

In a little, over 4 years your invested capital has gone pretty much nowhere, but 10 years later it would be worth $20,146.82 (5). So you could look at it as just staying the course would still put you ahead of the game and beat out inflation.

However, hindsight is 20/20, what if a percentage of your portfolio had $100k invested in an index fund and the stock market crash dropped your investment in this fund to $62k; that is a loss of 32%. Would you panic? Would you sell your shares and buy safer but lower return investments such as bonds?

What if you were about to retire around 2008-2009 and you had an investment account of $1 million. Most of it was invested in safer securities such as treasury bills and bonds, but a good percentage, let's say 30%, was still invested in stocks. The stock market crash just drops the stocks portion by 32%, so the $300k you had invested in stocks is now only worth $204k which was a loss of $96k.

This instantly affects your retirement plans, because you were planning on living off your $1 million which is now worth around $900k (plus don't forget about all those costs that your financial institution charges).

With the $1 million originally build-up you were going to apply the 4% rule that most financial planners advice to use when drawing money out of your account for retirement.

The 4% rule

The **4% rule** states that you should be able to live off 4% of your retirement income for 20 to 30 years. So, with a $1 million portfolio drawing 4% would be $40k out of your account in the first year. Your retirement account value would swing up and down based on market movement and which investments you are invested in (bonds, stocks, mutual funds, etc.)

Here is the problem with the 4% rule. If your investment dropped to $900k because of the stock market crash, a 4% withdrawal will only give you $36k instead of $40k. So if you still want that $40k you need to withdraw an additional 0.5%.

You might be thinking that this is not a big deal, because when the market is booming you will be able to take out less than 4% and in times of distress you might have to take out a little more than 4%, so it all evens out.

This brings me to the second issue I have with the 4% rule, which is that you are selling your assets for money. Think about a car you own which you are constantly stripping for money.

You start with a brand new or slightly used car that is paid for, so it's your property you use to drive to and from work.

Because you need money badly you start selling parts of your car every month. First, you start with your radio, then your speakers, and then your backseat. Before you know it your car will be worth nothing.

Now, you might think that's why we have bonds and annuities, but even with these securities, you need to make sure that they are inflation averse. There are certain annuities, however, that payout increasing payments.

When a shareholder invests for dividends, the investor does not have to sell their assets, because they will live off their dividends that the asset pays them. Also, many dividend companies still pay out an increasing dividend even during a market crash. Just look at the image below of PepsiCo dividend payments.

Figure 5.2 PepsiCo Stock Chart Starting From 2007. Source: Google Finance

Not only did PepsiCo continue to pay out quarterly dividends during the housing crisis of 2008-2009, but they also increased their quarterly dividend from 43 cents to 45 cents. They paid out a total dividend of $1.67 per share in 2008 and $1.78 in 2009. This is a dividend increase of 6.6%.

You might have a retirement plan and you decide that you will grow it to around $1 million at retirement age. Your retirement assets will mostly consist of safer investments. You decide to live off $50k per year from your $1 million nest egg.

Take a look at your buying power after 20 years based on a 3.5% inflation rate.

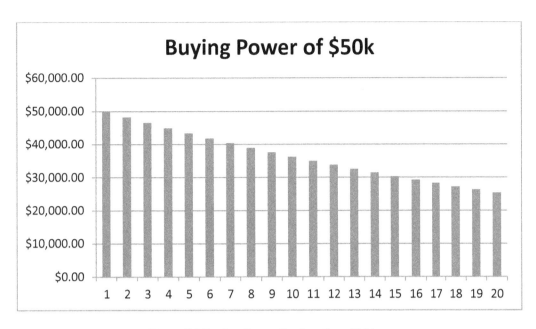

Figure 5.3 Buying Power Decline Over 20 Years

In year one you draw out $50,000, year two you still draw out $50,000 but your buying power has decreased to $48,250, because of inflation. In year 20, your $50,000 has a buying power of a little over $25,000. So your buying power is halved in 20 years.

If you have set up your investments to keep up with inflation, you should be able to increase the amount you withdraw while still maintaining your buying power. But many unexpected things happen in life, medical costs are rising, you might have to replace an old car that is starting to cost you too much to repair, home renovation, and more things we do not account for.

Women on average also live longer than men, this means that they will have to stretch their nest egg even longer.

As stated earlier, when investing in dividend-paying stocks, investors don't have to worry about selling the assets they own in their investment portfolio, because they will live off the dividend income generated. How much an investor needs to generate in dividend income to live prosperously is up to them.

I would recommend building up dividend income to twice the amount you make at your job.

Buy great companies

How do you determine what a great company is and how much should you pay for it? Is a great company one that is environmentally friendly? Is it a company that sells a lot of merchandise? How about a company that treats its customers and employees right?

A great company, in the context of buying it as an investment, is a company that **consistently** generates a healthy **net income**. Not only that, it should also be able to increase its net income year after year. The net income of a company is the bottom line, it's what's leftover after all the expenses, interest, and taxes have been deducted from the revenue the company generated.

Total revenue generated has an impact on the net income of a company. So, in order to increase its net income year after year, one thing a company can do is to increase its total revenue, which is the company's gross income from its sale of goods or services.

To increase revenue, a company can:

- Sell its product at a higher price
- Increase its customer base (ex. sell products in a different country)
- Sell more of the same product to existing customers
- Create new products to sell or buy existing ones from the competition

If a company can increase its total revenue while management efficiently keeps cost and other liabilities in check; the extra revenue generated from sales will have a positive impact on the **bottom line** (net income).

You want to look at total revenue and net income year over year for the last 5 or 10 years and see if the company has been able to **consistently** increase both. Focusing more on the last five years will give you a better picture of a company's recent performance.

If a company has been able to increase total revenue year over year by let's say 3%, but the net income has stayed flat, that could be concerning. It could be that management has been taking a bigger salary, the company might be taking on more debt, hiring on new employees, expanding the business, etc.

If total revenue is staying flat or slightly declining, but net income is increasing, that might be a concern, also. It could be that the company is losing market share to a competitor or the products or services they sell are losing customer appeal. So, management is doing some internal restructuring, to keep the company afloat.

Let's look at examples of two great companies and two other companies I would refrain from investing in.

Fastenal (**FAST**) is a company that sells industrial and construction supplies to businesses and retail customers. The company started as a partnership in 1967 and has been so successful that it has expanded beyond the US.

Take a look at both the Total Revenue and the Net Income graph:

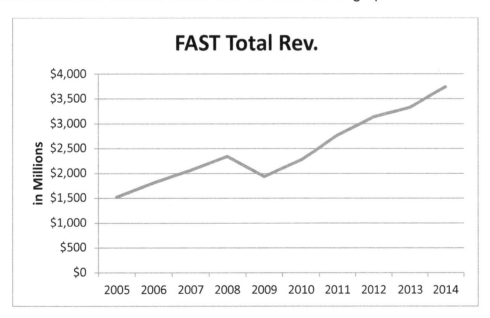

Figure 6.1 Fastenal Total Revenue 2005-2014

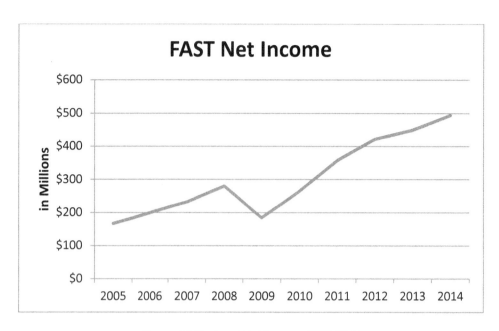

Figure 6.2 Fastenal Net Income 2005-2014

Both Total Revenue and Net Income have been growing at a steady pace. There was one year when both took a dip. This was in 2009 when the recession hit, but a great company can bounce back and continue generating a healthy income, because of its competitive advantage. Also, notice how both the Total Revenue and Net Income move in a symmetrical fashion. The increase in total revenue had an immediate impact on the bottom line (net income).

Let's look at the next one, Estee Lauder (**EL**), founded in the mid-nineties, a company that sells cosmetic products in high-end fashion stores. Their products are sold all over the world and they own brands such as Tom Ford and DKNY.

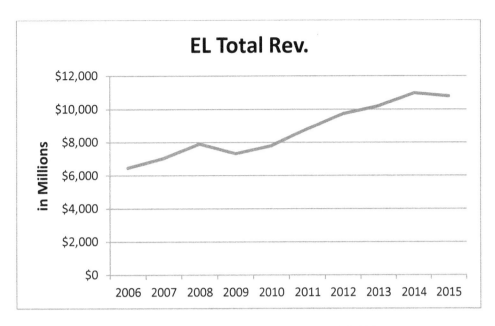

Figure 6.3 Estee Lauder Total Revenue 2006-2015

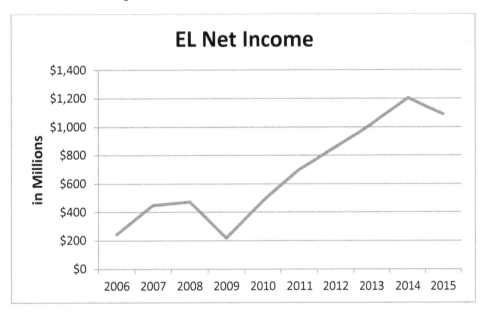

Figure 6.4 Estee Lauder Total Net Income 2006-2015

Total revenue is seeing a consistent increase year over year but look at the net income. It has taken off since 2009. What's happened is that they have been able to increase their profit margin from the single digits into double digits.

To calculate profit margin you take net income / total revenue.

Table 6.1 Estee Lauder Profit Margin 2008-2015

Estee Lauder	2008	2009	2010	2011	2012	2013	2014	2015
Total Revue	$7,911	$7,324	$7,796	$8,810	$9,714	$10,182	$10,969	$10,780
Net Income	$474	$218	$478	$701	$857	$1,020	$1,204	$1,089
Profit margin	5.99%	2.98%	6.13%	7.96%	8.82%	10.02%	10.98%	10.10%

Let's now look at two companies I would refrain from invest in, based on their performance for the past years.

Sprint (**S**) is a company that operates in the wireless communication industry, offering both wireless and wireline products to its customer base. Other competitors are companies like AT&T and Verizon.

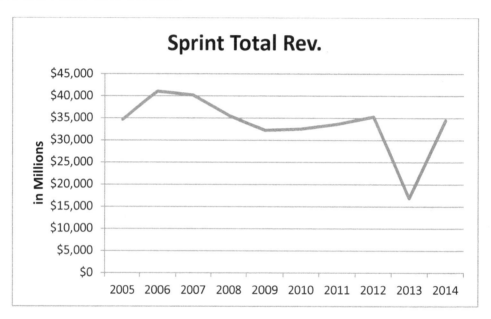

Figure 6.5 Sprint Total Revenue 2005-2014

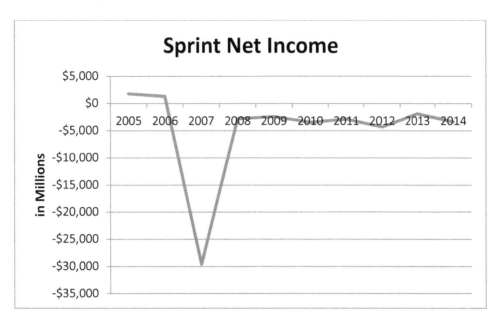

Figure 6.6 Sprint Net Income 2005-2014

Sprint's total revenue hit its peak at around $40 billion in 2006-2007 and has been on the decline since then. Sprint's net income is not any better. The company has been operating at a net loss since 2007. When a company performs with these kinds of numbers it will reflect in its stock price.

Let's look at American Airlines (**AAL**), a well-known airline of many frequent flyers. AAL also owns Us Airways and Envoy Aviation. American Airlines flies all over the world.

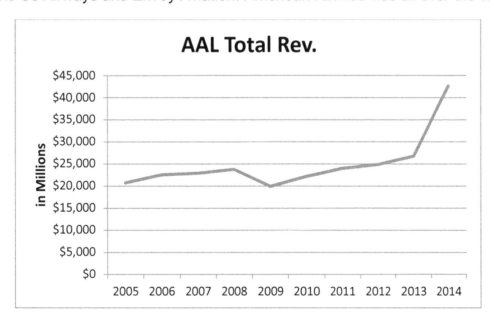

Figure 6.7 American Airlines Total Revenue 2005-2014

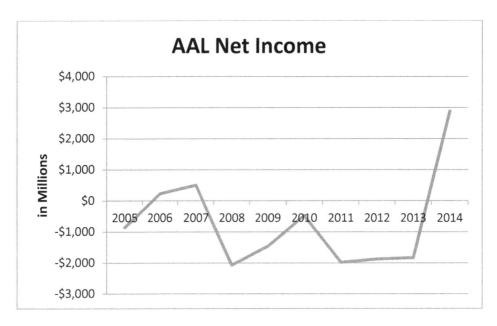

Figure 6.8 American Airlines Net Income 2005-2014

American Airline's total revenue doesn't look too bad; they took a hit during the recession, but have been able to increase their revenue since the recession.

Their net income, on the other hand, is nothing to brag about. They have generated a net loss for a good many years and just recently got back in the green. No consistency at all.

A company that only generates losses is a company that could eventually go bankrupt if management does not make drastic changes. A company like this might also be bought out by the competition. It could also be a company that is still in the growth phase. These are companies I avoid.

The last two examples were companies that both operated at a net loss for many years. The net loss itself is a dead giveaway for me not to invest in such a company, but what I'm looking for is consistency of growth. There might be a year or two where the company underperforms, but great companies can get back on track.

So what I look for is a **consistent upward trend** of increasing revenue and income.

Competitive advantage

A great company should have, as Warren Buffett has coined it, a moat. This is the competitive advantage a company has over its competition. This advantage allows the company to dominate its industry, to pull the company out of financial turmoil, and to keep customers constantly coming back for its products or services.

It's the unique path a company has carved for itself that sets them apart from the competition and it also breeds customer loyalty. If the customer wants this specific product or service, they can only get it from this company.

The competitive advantage, or moat, could be a brand name; like Colgate (**CL**) for toothpaste. It could also be Johnson & Johnson (**JNJ**) that sells brand name products like its baby lotion. Let's not forget Coke (**KO**), which has been selling pretty much the same soft drink for over 50 years.

A competitive advantage could also be a high barrier to entry in a specific market, or a geographical monopoly a company has.

There is no substitute for a company's moat, if you want to eat a Big Mac, you can only get it from McDonalds (**MCD**), the same goes for Pampers diapers from P&G (**PG**), or Gatorade from PepsiCo. (**PEP**).

One way to determine a company's moat is to ask yourself if the customer would buy a different product or service if the company increased its price. So if Coke increased the price of their bottles from $1 to $1.10, would the customers still buy coke or would they buy the off-brand?

There are many services or products offered that customers buy based on the price of the product alone. The business that can offer the lowest cost will get the customer. Commodities, such as sugar, cement, or cocoa are bought mostly based on price. The same goes for flights and automobiles. That's why these companies have historically been horrible investments.

When comparison shopping flights online, most people go with the cheapest option. Even though this is also mostly true for cars, there are a couple of car companies that have been able to create a moat for themselves. Think about a company like Ferrari S.p.A, which has carved out a niche for being a luxury sports car brand for rich people only.

The vast majority of car shoppers, however, are very price-aware when shopping for a car.

Also, there are a couple of companies that sell excellent products. These products are so entrenched in society that the companies that own these products have been able to sell the same product year after year, decade after decade, without making any or slight changes: Coke, Pepsi, Tide, Bounty, are some to name a few.

The Coca Cola Company has been selling the same Coke for decades now. Coca Cola does not have to do research and development or update their product which all cost money. All Coca Cola has to do is sell their product, something they do very well.

These products are **cash cows** and benefit shareholders greatly. I always look at owning companies that sell these types of products. It's a guaranteed dividend machine.

Just ask yourself this question: "Has this company been able to sell the same product for at least the last ten years?"

Responsible management

Always look for a company to invest in that has a good management team running operations. You won't be able to see what management does day by day, but there are other ways that you can check up on their performance. One telling sign is to see if the company can increase its shareholder equity, net income, and be able to keep debt in control and increase their profit margin.

The best way to check on management is to see how the company has performed in the past few years. This gives you an indication of how productive management is.

Stock buyback

I look for companies that buy their shares back. If you own shares of a company that buys their shares back, you have a couple of benefits working for you. First, your ownership in the company increases.

If a company has 1,000,000 shares outstanding and you own 10,000 shares of that company. You own 1% of the company (10,000/1,000,000)

If the company started buying their shares and there are now only 400,000 shares outstanding. You still own your 10,000 shares but your ownership in the company has just increased to 2.5% (10,000/400,000).

The second benefit is that you did not have to buy any additional shares or pay taxes for your ownership in the company to increase.

The third benefit is the company has been able to increase its earnings, which could potentially increase the price of the stock on the market.

Let's say this company generated $1 million in net income. The earnings of a company are the net income per share. So with $1 million in net income and 1 million shares outstanding, the earnings of the company are $1 per share ($1 million/1 million shares)

If the company bought their stocks and now had 400,000 shares outstanding and they still generated $1 million in net income, the earnings of the company are now $2.50 per share ($1 million/ 400,000 shares outstanding).

To see if a company is buying back its shares, all you have to do is look at the total amount of shares outstanding for the last 5 or 10 years. If you see the amount of shares outstanding decreasing, that means a company is buying back its shares.

See image below:

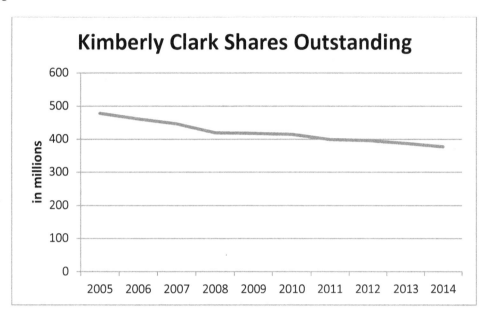

Figure 6.9 Kimberly Clark Stock Buyback 200-2014

As you can see a company as Kimberly Clark has steadily been buying back its shares year after year.

Pay off debt

Debt is not necessarily a bad thing. Companies often take on debt to expand their core business. Problems arise when a company takes on more debt than it can handle. Debt is also a major profit killer in economic downturns, which could leave your dividend in jeopardy to be cut or frozen.

The **debt to equity ratio** is a popular ratio used to figure out how much debt a company has in relation to its shareholder's equity.

D/E ratio= total liabilities/equity

A high debt to equity ratio is if a lot of debt is used to finance the company. There is no hard or fast rule, but I like to see a consistent D/E ratio **below 1**. Some industries, however, always have a higher D/E ratio.

Another way I also analyze a company's debt situation is by trying to figure out how many years it takes for a company to pay its total liabilities with the income it generates (before taxes). We want to see 5 years or less.

For example, McDonalds had a D/E ratio of 1.17 in 2014. I then take total liabilities/net income (before taxes) = 3.34 (21.4 billion/6.4 billion). So, McDonalds could pay off its debt in less than 4 years (additional interest expense not accounted for).

Return on equity

The **return on equity** formula is a great way to find excellent companies. ROE tells you how much net income is generated based on shareholders' equity. This is easy to calculate: ROE = Net Income/Shareholder Equity. The greater this number is, the more income a company has been able to generate using equity. ROE tells you how well management is working on taking equity and generating a healthy profit.

ROE is also a great indicator of a company with a competitive advantage because they will have a consistently high ROE.

If you had $20,000 and invested $10,000 each in two companies, your shareholder equity is $10,000 per company. Company A was able to generate an income of $1,000 and company B $3,000.

Your ROE for company A is 10% ($1,000/$10,000). Company B ROE is 30%.

Based on this example you can already guess that company B is the winner because it has been able to generate more income, but we're not done yet.

Both companies decide to pay out 50% in dividends and the rest is retained in the company (**retained earnings**).

Company A's dividend is $500 Company B's dividend is $1,500. The retained earnings are added to shareholders' equity.

Company A $10,000+$500= $10,500

Company B $10,000+$1,500= $11,500

The next year both companies had the same ROE, 10% and 30%.

Company A generated $1,050 (10%) and B $3,450 (30%) and both paid out a 50% dividend again.

Company A $525, Company B $1,725.

The rest is retained in the company and added to shareholder equity.

Company A: $10,500+$525= $11,025

Company B: $11,500 + $1,725 = $13,225

As you can see, not only is Company B able to pay a higher dividend, they are also able to grow their net income and shareholder equity at a higher rate than company A.

This is why you always want to invest in companies that have a consistently high ROE. Look for companies that generate a ROE in the double digits.

Because companies can manipulate ROE in their favor, I also look at the Return on invested capital (ROIC). This shows how profitable a company is based on its invested capital. The calculation is (net income – dividends) / total capital.

I look for ROE and ROIC in double digits.

Table 6.2 Genuine Parts Company ROE and ROIC

Genuine Parts Co	2010	2011	2012	2013	2014
ROE	17.6%	20.3%	22.4%	21.6%	21.4%
ROIC	14.8%	17.7%	19.5%	18.5%	17.8%

The annual report

Every single company that is publicly traded is obligated to report its performance to its shareholders. Companies post their annual and quarterly reports for their investors on their website.

Annual reports, also called a Form 10-k, can be found online or you can request them from the company, also.

Annual reports are structured; they usually start with a shareholders letter from the CEO on how the company has performed the last quarters.

Then you get a detailed overview of the company's business, risk factors, and so forth.

There are plenty of companies that have a habit of beautifying their annual reports. So, whenever you're looking at an annual report, don't be fooled by all the smiling faces, skip past all the pretty pictures and smiling faces and go directly to the necessary information, which are the financial reports.

Income Statement	Balance Sheet	Cash Flow Statement
Revenue Expenses Net Income	Assets Liabilities Shareholder's Equity	Cash flow from operations Cash flow from investing Cash flow from Financing Net increase/decrease in cash

Figure 6.10 Publicly Traded Companies Financial statements

These three reports (income statement, balance sheet, and cash flow statement) have all the company's financial data you need.

The income statement shows the profitability of a company for a specified date range.

The balance sheet lists the assets a company has, such as buildings and equipment, liabilities (short term and long term), and the equity of the shareholders. This report always needs to be balanced.

The cash flow statement gives you a picture of how the company is using its cash to operate the business.

Instead of browsing through all these annual reports for different companies, I use sites like Yahoo Finance, MSN Money, and Morningstar.

Morningstar is my go-to site for financial information. It's always best to double-check the financial numbers on Morningstar to the financial numbers in the annual reports, but I've noticed that Morningstar is highly accurate.

The benefit of Morningstar is that it shows the important financial metrics of publicly traded companies for the last 5 or ten years. So you don't have to page through different annual reports of the same company to make sense of all the numbers. This **speeds up** the process of analyzing companies.

You don't have to be an accountant to read through these financial reports, but it does help to have a basic understanding of them.

Analyzing the dividend

When analyzing the dividend a company pays out, the first thing you need to look at is if the company has paid out a dividend in at least 10 years. The reason for this is that it will show consistency in paying dividends even in times of economic downturns. Secondly, the company needs to have increased the dividend on average **faster than inflation** or at least keep up with it. This will allow your dividend to keep its buying power.

Third, look at the company's earnings per share and compare it to the dividend paid out to shareholders. Your dividend is paid out of the earnings of the company.

If a company made $1 million in net income and had 500,000 shares outstanding the earnings per share would be $2 ($1,000,000/500,000). The company decides to pay out $500,000 of the net income out as a dividend. Per-share this is $1 ($500,000/500,000 shares).

If you owned 800 shares you would receive one dollar for each share you owned as a dividend, so that would be $800 total in dividend income.

A company that can increase its net income or earnings per share, will also be able to increase its dividend if the board of directors agrees on increasing the dividend.

The movement of the stock price on the stock market is influenced by many factors such as fear and greed of investors, but it is also influenced by the company's earnings.

Companies post their earnings for the quarter. If a company misses its earnings goal by even a few pennies, it could hurt the stock price.

If the company was able to beat its projected earnings, there is a likely chance that the price of the stock will increase.

An increase in earnings is especially important to investors that are investing to receive dividends. Since dividends are paid out of earnings, which are net income per share, if the earnings increase, board directors will increase the dividends also to keep their shareholders happy.

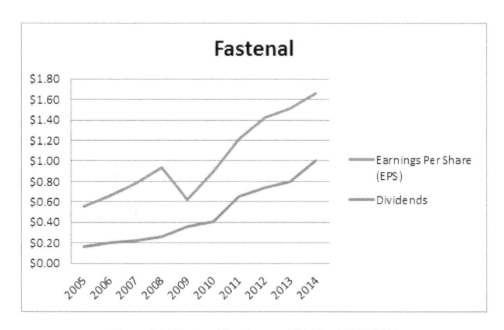

Figure 6.11 Fastenal Earnings and Dividend 2005-2014

Fastenal has been able to grow its dividend above 20% on average year after year in the last 5 and ten years.

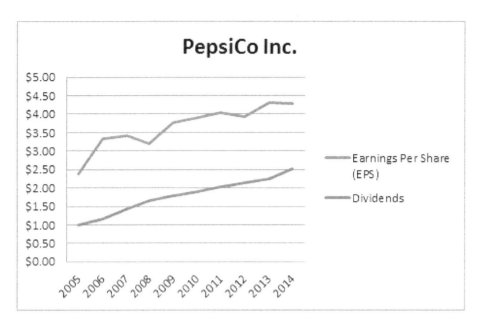

Figure 6.12 PepsiCo Earnings and Dividend 2005-2014

PepsiCo has been able to grow its dividend by 7.3% on average year after year in the last 5 years and 10% on average in the last 10 years. Not as spectacular as Fastenal, but it's growing faster than inflation and that's all that matters.

Many investors, like Warren Buffett, like using a discount model to project future earnings. This will give them the confidence to buy a stock at a certain price. To me, a discount model leaves too much margin of error. You can never predict the future, but I can guess by looking at the past performance of the companies I want to invest in. That is why consistency is extremely important. A company like Fastenal has been able to consistently grow its earnings around 14% on average every year for the last ten years.

They've also consistently been able to keep their ROE and ROIC above 20% and also have a low amount of debt. The company also has a competitive advantage. It's the consistency of companies that give me the **confidence** to invest in them.

If I am analyzing companies, but notice that their earnings were erratic and their ROE and ROIC were inconsistent I would not be confident investing in the company.

Payout ratio
Looking at the Fastenal and PepsiCo graph, again, you can see that companies that increase their earnings can safely increase their dividends also. The amount of dividend a company pays out compared to the earnings is called the **Payout ratio**.

For the year 2014, PepsiCo had total earnings per share of $4.27. It paid $2.53 out as a dividend. The payout ratio is 59.25% ($2.53/$4.27).

A good payout ratio depends on the company and the industry it is in. Some industries like REITs and utility stocks have historically had a high payout ratio.

I typically look for companies that have a payout ratio of 60% or less. Consistency, as always is key.

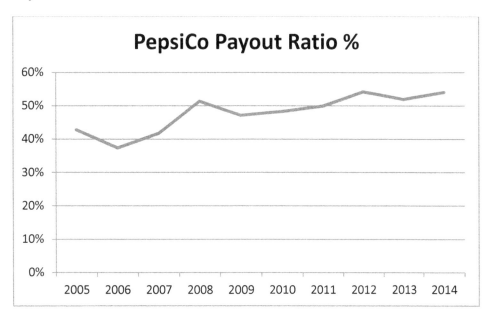

Figure 6.13 PepsiCo Payout Ratio 200-2014

Pepsi has been able to **consistently** keep the payout ratio below 60% in the last 10 years, even through the Great Recession.

If you notice that a payout ratio keeps climbing and is getting closer to 100%, it means that almost all of its earnings are paid out as a dividend. This is not good, because a company needs to retain a certain amount of earnings to invest back in the business.

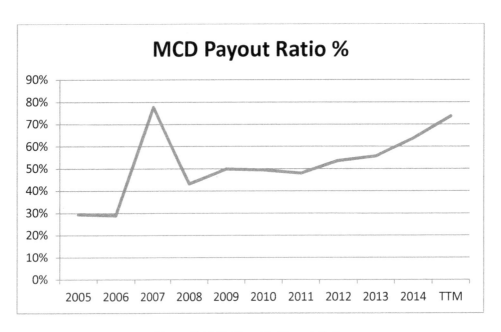

Figure 6.14 McDonalds Payout Ratio

Looking at McDonald's payout ratio, you can see that their payout ratio has seen a steady increase from 30% in 2005 to over 70% in 2015. The past few years McDonalds has struggled to acquire new customers and they have been losing customers to healthier fast-food restaurants and shops like Subway and Chipotle.

They've seen their total revenue and gross profit take a small dip in the last couple of years. They've been increasing their dividend at a higher percentage than their earnings growth. This is not a deal-breaker, but it is something to pay attention to.

Dividend yield

The **dividend yield** is the percentage of dividend you receive compared to what the price of the stock is. So, if a stock sells on the market for $40 and the dividend per stock is $1, your dividend yield is 2.5% ($1/$40). Higher yield is better, right? Not necessarily. Usually with stocks that pay a high dividend yield, 5% or up, they either grow their dividend at a slower pace or there might be something going on with the company that made their stock price drop (like missing their earnings goal by a few pennies).

The lower the share price drops, the higher the dividend yield will be. So, in our previous example, if the dividend is still at $1 a share and the share price tumbles to $25, now the dividend yield is 4%.

Not all, but many companies that pay a high dividend also have a high payout ratio.

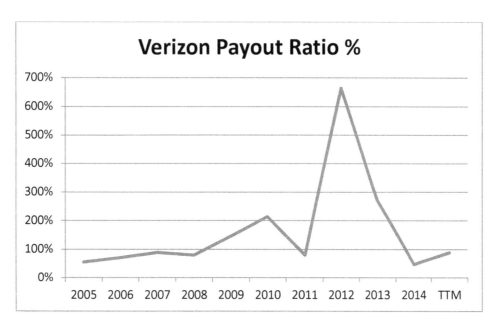

Figure 6.15 Verizon Payout Ratio

Verizon has a 5.03% dividend yield and an average payout ratio of 90%. This means that they payout 90% of their earnings out to shareholders in the form of dividends.

They have been growing their dividend at a rate of 2.9% over the last years. 2.9% is not flattering, but one benefit with high dividend-yielding stocks is that you get a higher dividend income upfront that you can use to reinvest or buy other stocks.

So what is better, higher yield low growth or lower yield high growth? I lean toward lower yield faster growth, but honestly, I have both in my investment portfolio.

Keep in mind, however, that if the economy goes through a slump and stock prices start declining across the board, many stocks will have a high yield. This is the optimal scenario to buy great companies and receive a high yielding dividend.

Many companies with a competitive advantage can increase their dividends without having to sell more products or services or find new customers to sell to, even if their customer base is small.

For example, a company that sells potato chips sells an 8 oz. bag for $1. They have a customer base of 100,000 people that love their potato chips. Every customer just buys one bag, which gives this company a total revenue of $100k. Total expenses for one bag end up being 80 cents, which leaves the company a net income of $20,000 (20 cents x 100,000 bags sold).

The company decides to pay out a 50% dividend, so shareholders receive a total of $10,000 in dividends.

The following year's cost per bag has gone up to 90 cents, the company decides to pass the cost on to its customers and sells the same 8 oz. bag for $1.15. They still have the same customer base that buys one bag. Now their total revenue is $115,000. The company's net income is $25,000. They stick with the 50% payout ratio and end up paying $12,500 total in dividends. The company was able to increase its dividend by 25%, without having acquired new customers or selling more potato chip bags.

So, whenever you go into your local grocery store and notice that the prices on your favorite products have increased, now you know why.

Companies with a competitive advantage can raise their prices year after year and also raise the dividends they pay out, without acquiring new customers.

We've looked at a couple of metrics that can be used to analyze a company. Are these the only metrics? No, but these performance metrics give you a high-level overview of how the company is performing. If anything seems off, I can always dive in deeper and comb through the financial statements. This, however, is something that I rarely do; because that's way too boring.

I just stick to the high-level metrics, because anything that might affect performance in a bad way will filter to the top and I will notice it either by the P/E ratio dropping, the price of the stock tumbling, weak earnings report, dip in revenue or net income, high debt level or any other bad circumstances that could pop up.

I also lean on a company's competitive advantage pulling it out of any business turmoil it might go through and I keep an eye on the 5 to 10 years performance.

How much to pay
You go to your local grocery store and you see your favorite chocolate candy bar selling for $3, you are used to buying it cheaper than $3, so you decide not to purchase it that day.

You go back to the store after one week and you notice that the price of the same chocolate candy bar is now on sale for $1. You freak out and start loading up on chocolate candy bars because you've never seen it this cheap.

That's the same way you are going to be buying dividend stocks when you can get them at a **deep discount**. How much you pay for a stock depends on the value of the stock itself. You don't just buy a stock because you like the company. You should only buy if the stock is trading at a deep discount compared to its value.

Right now Walmart has a market cap of $189 billion and Chevron has a market cap of $167 billion. If I gave you $190 billion today and told you to buy the company that's the better deal, which one would you buy? Why?

Would you buy Chevron because it looks cheaper compared to Walmart? Always look at buying stocks as if you're buying the whole company. If you take that perspective, you will be more diligent in your research on deciding which company's stock to buy.

Also, if you wouldn't buy the whole company if you had the capital, don't even think about buying even one share in the company.

To figure out which of the two companies we would like to buy and how much we want to pay for it, we need to decide the value of a company first. There are two ways: book value or net income.

The book value is the tangible worth of the company and this is also what shareholders would get if the company gets liquidated (sold). Book value is calculated as assets – liabilities. Book value may look like shareholders equity, but it only contains tangible assets that can be sold. Intangible assets like goodwill or brand recognition cannot be sold.

Net income is the second and my most favorite way of valuing a company. The amount of income a company generates tells me how much I am willing to pay for it. Since we are looking to invest in profitable businesses that should not get liquidated, we will use the net income method of valuing a business.

Let's scale it back a little bit with a fun short story. A group of kids in your neighborhood are very assertive and entrepreneurial. They started their own lemonade business, where they've set up lemonade stands in the local community.

All year round they meet plenty of thirsty customers and they can generate $10,000 in net profit. They sell lemonade for 50 cents a glass and make 25 cents profit. So they are selling more than 100 glasses a day to reach that $10k profit.

After doing this for a year, they are getting tired of standing outside in rain, sleet or snow and would rather be sitting at home playing video games all day (games they bought with their lemonade money of course).

You offer to buy the lemonade business from them and have your nephews running the day to day operations. They got in a huddle and did some quick math.

If the lemonade business makes them $10,000 a year profit, it would be foolish to sell it for less than that amount, because they will have incurred a major loss. If they sell it for $10,000 they haven't made any profit, because they can do those numbers in a year.

All things being equal, if their expenses and profit stay the same year after year, they decide to sell the business for $100,000, which is 10 years' worth of profits. So the young entrepreneurs decided on $100,000, they think that amount will buy them video games for a lifetime.

Now you, on the other hand, want to get the business as cheap as possible. If you can get it for $5,000 you will be up 100% the first year. Because you spend $5,000 and the business generated $10,000. If you can buy their business for $10,000, you are also a winner, because you will have made your money back in just one year. Everything after year one is just pure profit.

You were eventually able to negotiate the price down to $50,000, which means that you will make all your money back in year 5 or a 20% immediate return of your investment ($10,000/$50,000). After year five, everything you earn is just pure profit and you can use the money to buy a different business.

There is a specific formula that investors use, called the **P/E ratio**. It shows you how much money you pay for $1 profit a company generates. P stands for price and E stands for earnings.

We paid $50,000 (P) for the lemonade company and the company had a net income, or earnings, of $10,000 (E). So you take the earnings and divide that by the price to get the P/E ratio: $50,000/$10,000 = 5. For every 5 dollars, you spend you bought one dollar in profit.

The same way we valued the young entrepreneurs' lemonade business is the same way we will evaluate the big businesses on the stock market, like Walmart and Chevron. Don't forget that when we invest we are looking at our initial return and how many years it will take to get our original investment back.

We're going to do two things, we're taking the market cap of the companies, which is the total value of the company on the stock market and break it down to a single share price and we will take the net income and break it down to income for a single share.

The market cap for Walmart is $189 billion, they have 3.20 billion shares outstanding, so to break it down to a single share price we take: $189 billion / 3.20 billion shares outstanding = $59.08.

$59.08, is also the price that you will see on the stock market when people are talking about the share price of Walmart.

Walmart generated $14.912 billion in net income. To break it down to one share we take $14.912 billion / 3.20 billion shares outstanding = $4.66. This $4.66 is the net income per share, but investors also call it earnings per share (EPS). The earnings per share are nothing more than the total net income divided by shares outstanding.

Now to get to our P/E ratio, we take our EPS and divide that by the price: $59.08/$4.66= 12.68. For every $12.68 you spend you bought $1 in Walmart profit.

Another way to look at it is you had an initial 7.9% initial rate of return ($1/$12.68), or if Walmart made the same income year after year, it would take 12.68 years to get your investment money back.

As an investor you want to get your initial investment back as fast as possible, that's why you should only buy companies that have a low P/E ratio.

But what is a low P/E ratio? It depends on the stock market, the economy, the industry your company is in, and on the average P/E the company has been trading in the past years.

I've noticed that most companies I keep an eye on are trading at a P/E ranging from 7 to 75. Most investors like buying companies that are trading at a P/E of 20 or less. I only buy companies trading at a **P/E of 15 or less**.

Whenever the economy is prospering and people feel optimistic, they spend money more freely and the stock market reflects this behavior. Companies start trading at higher P/E ratios of 30 and up because investors bid up the price of the stock. This is when the market as a whole is overvalued.

For example, company ABC is selling for $100 a share and has earnings of $4, for a P/E ratio of 25. Investors start bidding up the price of the stock to $140. The earnings are still at $4, which gives us a P/E ratio of 35. This to me is too high of a P/E ratio, like I said earlier I only buy at P/E ratios of 15 or less.

The opposite also holds true, whenever the economy tanks, like during the great depression, people get real pessimistic about the economy and start selling their stocks and investments because they feel like the sky is falling.

The stock market goes up and everybody jumps on the bandwagon and bids up the prices of stocks. The stock market is overvalued and the bubble is about to burst. Then the stock market tanks or corrects itself and everybody tries to jump off the ship and tries to save themselves, now the market is undervalued.

So in this case company ABC went from $140 a share at its peak and tumbled down to $130, $119, $101, $80, $58, and then to $40. If earnings per share is still at $4, now the P/E ratio is at 10.

Everybody tried to get out of the market as quickly as possible because stock prices were falling. You will now see P/E ratios in the single digits.

It is at this moment that I shift into second gear and start buying companies like my life depended on it. I'm like a kid in a candy store and the owner tells me that I can have all the candy I can put my hands on in the next 30 minutes.

Remember, it's the shareholders who trade these stocks back and forth. The underlying company still is fundamentally sound and will generate profits and dividends for its shareholders.

Also, most investors don't trade their stocks frequently. The average volume of shares that have been trading daily for Walmart stock is about 11.72 million, compared to 3.20 billion shares outstanding. That is 0.37% of total shares that are trading daily. The other 99.63% of shares are owned by investors who just sit on their shares and collect the dividend.

Walmart P/E was under 15 in 2009. Also, with a lower P/E ratio I can buy more stocks, which will give me more dividends.

If I had $2,000 to spend and I bought company ABC at $140 a share I would only be able to buy 14 whole shares, but if I bought the company at $40 a share, I would have bought 50 shares. Instead of getting 14 cash dividends, I now get 50 cash dividends.

Going back to our Walmart vs Chevron example, it would be tedious to constantly have to calculate the market cap, share price, P/E ratio, and EPS. Luckily most of this information is readily available and you can just look at the P/E ratio without having to think about the calculation.

	Company name	Price	Change	Chg %	d | m | y	Earnings per share	P/E ratio	Mkt Cap	Dividend	Dividend yield
WMT	Wal-Mart Stores, ...	59.66	+0.60	1.02%		4.66	12.79	189.04B	1.92	3.32

Figure 6.16 Walmart Investment Metrics. Source: Google Finance

For example, Google Finance already has these numbers calculated for you. You can also add all the dividend calculations if you want to. Let's skip calculating Chevron's EPS and P/E ratio and let's just pull it from our online source.

	Company name	Price	Change	Chg %	d | m | y	Earnings per share	P/E ratio	Mkt Cap	Dividend	Dividend yield
CVX	Chevron Corporation	89.71	+0.86	0.97%		4.60	19.49	167.22B	4.21	4.82

Figure 6.17 Chevron Investment Metrics. Source: Google Finance

Based on the P/E ratios alone I would buy Walmart instead of Chevron.

Keep in mind that dividends are paid out of earnings and if you look at both Walmart and Chevron you see that Chevron is paying a higher dividend. Without looking at other factors, I would still buy Walmart over Chevron.

A lower P/E ratio trumps the higher dividend.

One caveat, when analyzing REITs you should not use the EPS to calculate the P/E ratio, you should use the FFO (funds from operations), or better yet the AFFO (adjusted funds from operations). Your calculation will look like this: P/FFO or P/AFFO.

When to sell

You will hear good news about a company and the stock price will reflect this by going up. You will also hear bad news because a company might have missed its quarterly projected earnings by a few pennies and the stock price will tumble down or there might be some so-called financial expert who will tell you to buy a stock because it's about to sign a major contract which will boost sales.

It's best not to pay too much attention to all this noise and focus on the financial data.

When it comes to selling stocks, I only sell if a company stops paying the dividend, the company fundamentally changes for the worse, or if the dividend has not kept up with inflation.

If a company stops paying dividends, it tells me that the business is in some kind of financial trouble and I need to investigate. Companies keep their shareholders happy when they pay out dividends constantly. It's a major problem if the company stops paying out dividends, the stock will most likely also drop in price.

Not too long ago, I broke some of my own rules when it comes to buying dividend stocks and purchased stocks in a company called American Realty Capital Properties (ARCP). This was a monthly dividend-paying company, but it did not have at least a 10-year track record of paying increased dividends.

I received my first dividend when the pay date arrived, but the following dividends never arrived.

Management at ARCP was cooking the books and when this was found out all hell broke loose. The dividend was eliminated, senior management left the company, and shareholders were angry.

Throughout this whole debacle, the stock price continued to decline and it took a new management team and a change of company name to bring the company back on track.

The company ended up reinstated its dividend 10 months after paying the last one. Looking back I could've invested the money in a better way. But whenever you make a mistake and believe me you will make mistakes, just learn from it and move on. No use crying over spilled milk.

Sometimes companies fundamentally change by neglecting what they are good at or known for and instead jump into a new market. If a company you invested in is in the chocolate chip cookies selling business and all of a sudden jumps into fashion design and puts all of its energy and resources in building that up, it might not be the best use of resources.

There are quite a few companies that buy out competitors or try something new. PepsiCo, for example, sells many different products. Besides the Pepsi soft drink, they also sell Lays potato chips, Quaker oatmeal, Doritos, and more. They have a wide assortment of products, but they stay in the consumer staples industry. They don't stray away from what they do best.

If a company has not been able to grow its dividend fast enough, you should either sell it or collect the dividend you receive and purchase other companies with it.

Whenever I am not buying companies at a P/E of 15 or less, I just sit back and collect dividends. Being patient and waiting for the right opportunities to buy is a skill in itself.

As long as you follow the rules for selling dividend stocks, you will be able to tune out the noise. The worst thing you can do is constantly buy and sell your stocks because this will hurt your overall return.

Sitting still, not doing anything, and waiting for the right time to buy is a skill you will learn. Sometimes it can take months or years before you get the opportunity to buy a company you've been eyeing like a hawk at a low P/E ratio.

The fear of losing all your money
I've noticed that people have two fears, either the companies they invest in going bankrupt, whereby they believe they will lose all their money, or the stock market crashing.

Let's look at the first fear and how I deal with it. I only invest in high quality stable blue-chip companies that are not likely to go belly-up and have been paying a consistent dividend for at least **10 years**. Companies like Kimberly Clark, PepsiCo, and Coca Cola to name a few. The chances of companies like these going bankrupt are not very likely, because of their competitive advantage.

To lower my risk even further, I invest in at least 30 great companies and with the dividends, I receive from them I buy even more high-quality companies. By sticking to my rules I don't even let companies that I invest in get up to a point of going bankrupt, because I would have sold my shares before that happens. Signs that you need to look at to see how the company is performing: revenue or net income declining, high debt, dividend cuts or freezes and more (re-read the performance metrics I discussed earlier).

My biggest hint at selling a company, before everything else goes bad, is if the company stops paying a dividend, that's an immediate death sentence. The reason for this is, if a company performs good or even mediocre it can keep on paying a dividend even if they might not increase the dividend amount by much.

However, if a company that has paid a dividend for at least 10 years suddenly stops paying one, it tells me that they are having financial issues and more bad news might come to light soon. The companies' financial performance is what I use to keep myself from becoming fearful.

The second reason people are fearful is because of a stock market crash. When the market crashes people end up selling their investments at a **capital loss** turning their **unrealized** income in **realized** income.

This is a fear you get over by accepting that the market **will** crash, there are periods when people are optimistic about the market and the stock market as a whole becomes overvalued. Then there are other periods when people are pessimistic about the market as a whole and they want to sell all or some of their investments and the market becomes oversold.

I wait for periods when the market is trending downwards (bear market) or crashes because I can buy these high-quality companies at bargain prices which makes me able to buy more shares for my money, which also ends up giving me more dividends. Keep in mind that most likely, the underlying companies are still performing great.

It is the shareholders that own the stocks who are fearful and start selling, making the stock value tumble to a low P/E.

For example, around the time the market crashed, back in 2009, anywhere from 35 million to 165 million of Walmart shares were trading (mostly being sold) daily. That's still a minuscule amount of shares traded compared to the total shares Walmart had outstanding, which was 3.95 billion, that investors just held in their portfolios during the stock market crash. 165 million / 3.95 billion = 4.2% of stocks trading. It is this 4.2% that impacted the price of the stock.

Also, the best time for a company to start buying their shares back is during a crash, because they can buy them at a deep discount.

Locating dividend-paying stocks

One way to find dividend-paying stocks is to look at products or services you come in contact with throughout the day.

After you wake up you go to the bathroom to brush your teeth (Colgate), you take a shower and wash your hair with Head & Shoulders (Procter & Gamble). Before heading to work you eat a sandwich (Flower Foods). At work, you use your favorite calculator (Texas Instruments) to turn some calculations into a graph and during lunch, you head over to Taco Bell (Yum Brands) for a chalupa and burrito.

You will be neglecting plenty of high-quality dividend-paying companies if you just looked at products you or your friends and family use. So, another way to find dividend-paying stocks is to use an online stock screener. Google Finance and Finviz.com have screeners that you can use to screen for dividend-paying stocks. Just do a quick google search for stock screeners and you should be able to find plenty more.

Here is a list of 36 high-quality dividend-paying companies that you need to take a look at.

Table 6.3 List of High-Quality Dividend Paying Companies

Ticker	Company
DOV	Dover Corporation
EMR	Emerson Electric Company
WMT	Wal-Mart Stores, Inc.
AXP	American Express Company
TROW	T. Rowe Price Group, Inc.
XOM	Exxon Mobil Corporation
EV	Eaton Vance Corporation
GPC	Genuine Parts Company
PM	Philip Morris International Inc
CVX	Chevron Corporation
JNJ	Johnson & Johnson
MMM	3M Company
TXN	Texas Instruments Incorporated
MO	Altria Group, Inc.
FAST	Fastenal Company
SBSI	Southside Bancshares, Inc.
UL	Unilever
OHI	Omega Healthcare Investors, Inc

Ticker	Company
CL	Colgate-Palmolive Company
MCD	McDonald's Corporation
FLO	Flowers Foods, Inc.
CLX	Clorox Company
KO	Coca-Cola Company
ADP	Automatic Data Processing, Inc.
EL	Estee Lauder Companies, Inc.
MKC	McCormick & Company
PG	Procter & Gamble Company
PEP	PepsiCo, Inc.
COST	Costco Wholesale Corporation
NKE	Nike, Inc.
YUM	Yum! Brands, Inc.
HSY	The Hershey Company
WPC	W.P. Carey Inc. REIT
O	Realty Income Corporation
RAVN	Raven Industries, Inc.
KMB	Kimberly-Clark Corporation

Once I've found a great company that I want to buy, but it is trading at a high P/E ratio, I add it to my **watch list**. This is a list of all the stocks you are keeping an eye on. It also has performance and fundamental information, like the P/E ratio.

You should be able to create a watch list in your brokerage account. Google Finance also has a watch list feature called Portfolios.

Rules are meant to be broken

Do I stick to all the rules I listed? No, life is no fun if you don't break the rules. I sometimes break the rules for some companies but in moderation. I might look at a company like Disney (**D**) or Chubb (**CB**) that has a low dividend yield of 1% but has a great dividend growth rate. I'm also very careful about businesses that sell commodities, but if I can find one that is holding a monopoly status as its competitive advantage, I might look into purchasing a few shares.

Diversification

I diversify my dividend portfolio based on the ten US stock market sectors:

Consumer staples

This sector consists of products consumers use on an everyday basis. Even in an economic downturn, people will keep using them as they are always in demand. They consist of: beverages, food products, household products, personal products, and tobacco products.

Example of some companies: P&G, KMB, PM, EL, CL, PEP, KO

Consumer discretionary

These are the non-essential products or services that consumers could live without. If the economy is doing badly, people cut back on consumer discretionary products. They consist of: media, auto components, hotels, cruises, restaurants, vacation resorts, apparel, and cars.

Examples: DIS, YUM, COST, MCD, WMT, FAST, GPC

Energy

Energy companies consist of the production or supply of energy worldwide.

Example: KMI

Healthcare

There are a variety of companies in the healthcare sector: drug manufacturers, biotechnology, healthcare providers and services, medical appliances and equipment, and medical research. People always require medical aid, so this is a sector to keep an eye on.

Example: JNJ, PFE, ABBV

Financials

When you hear financials, you immediately think about banks. But this sector also consists of insurance, REITs, asset management, investment brokerage, and credit services. Companies in this sector do well when interest rates are low.

Example: AXP, TROW, CB, O

Utilities

Companies in this sector mostly carry a large amount of debt. These are electric utilities, gas utilities, water utilities, and multi utilities. These are often considered boring companies to invest in.

Example: AVA, SJI, WTR

Telecommunication services

Telecommunication services companies have set up elaborate infrastructures that give us the ability to communicate with our family and friends all over the world. The biggest section is wireless communication.

Example: VZ, T

Materials

The materials sector consists of raw materials that are harvested, refined, extracted, discovered and processed. These materials could be chemicals, metals, paper, construction material, and containers. The materials sector is highly dependent on the demand for their products which goes through cycles.

Example: APD, XOM, CVX, HP

Industrial goods

This sector, also highly dependent on demand, consists of different companies in different categories: aerospace & defense, airlines, machinery, construction, railroads, electrical equipment, commercial supplies & services, building products, and industrial conglomerates.

Example: DOV, EMR, GE, CAT

Information Technology

Tech stocks are favorite stocks of many investors because they are mostly growth stocks. People also like being associated with the coolest tech companies that are creative and always push the limit of what is possible. Competition is extremely high in information technology and it's not unusual to see today's cool companies be tomorrow's forgotten relics.

Many tech companies also don't pay a dividend, because they'd rather use the money to grow the company. The information technology sector consists of software, hardware, IT services, communication equipment, internet services, and semiconductors.

Example: MSFT, TXN, QCOM, CSCO, IBM

Weight by sector

Whenever you build a portfolio of securities, such as stocks and bonds, you diversify it and allocate weight based on your risk tolerance level. Someone younger is usually more aggressive and allocates more capital in high risk, high reward stocks. But someone who is less risky might focus more on safer investments such as bonds and annuities.

My portfolio weighted by sector:

Sector	Weight
Consumer staples	20%
Consumer discretionary	18%
Financials	17%
Healthcare	14%
Industrials	10%
Information technology	6%
Utilities	5%
Materials	5%
Telecom services	3%
Energy	2%
Total	100%

This is my portfolio weight by sector for my dividend stock portfolio. To be honest, I haven't been aggressively paying attention to it, but I always keep this in the back of my mind.

If I had to start from scratch and had $10,000 to spend, I would use 20%, or $2,000, and buy different consumer staples companies with that money. I would then take $1,800 and by different consumer discretionary companies, etc. I would then have my portfolio weighted by sector.

Consumer staples hold the highest percentage because it consists of companies that sell products that have a competitive advantage and sell well even when the economy is down.

Consumer discretionary, even though it does worse in an economic downturn, I still make this a large percentage of my portfolio, because it consists of many companies that have competitive advantages.

Finance also makes a large portion of my portfolio, focused on REITs, local banks, and credit services.

I would like to make healthcare a larger percentage of my portfolio, but there are not that many healthcare companies that qualify based on my rules.

I am careful with industrial, basic materials, and energy companies because most of the companies in these sectors are highly price-sensitive and cyclical. Many of these companies compete to be the lowest-cost producer and price, therefore, becomes the biggest factor that drives performance.

Utilities and telecom services also get a low percentage point in my dividend portfolio. High debt and high payout ratios make me keep these sectors to a minimum in my portfolio.

Information technology also gets a low ranking in my portfolio. Most of the companies in this sector are overvalued because people bid up the stock price too high. These companies most often don't pay a dividend. Consistency is also an issue because these companies are so competitive that they have to be creative and change with the times. This makes it harder for an investor to analyze a company that constantly changes.

For example, a "boring" blue-chip company like Phillip Morris sells one of the most well-known consumer staple products, called Marlboro.

I'm pretty sure 30 years from now PM will still sell Marlboro successfully. It's these kinds of stable companies which give me the confidence to invest in them.

Tech companies, on the other hand, change quite frequently and they come and go faster than I can keep up with them. Microsoft started as a software company that made money by selling and licensing out its products. Windows is what immediately comes to mind when thinking of Microsoft.

But in the following years, Microsoft has jumped in the gaming industry, phone hardware, cloud computing, and other avenues to keep up with the competition. Even though I have bought shares in Microsoft, it is hard to imagine what this company will look like 30 years from now.

The S&P 500 is weighted like this:

Sector	Weight
Information technology	21.14%
Financials	16.66%
Healthcare	14.67%
Consumer discretionary	13.08%
Industrials	10.05%
Consumer staples	9.69%
Energy	6.68%
Materials	2.85%
Utilities	2.82%
Telecom Services	2.36%
Total	100.00%

This is also what your portfolio looks like if you invest in an index fund like the popular VFINX. My biggest gripe with this weight by sector is that Information technology has way too much weight. When the stock market corrects itself, the information technology sector will be one that will be affected the most, especially since it is overvalued.

Consumer staples, the sector that performs well even in a downturn and consists of many companies with competitive advantages, has not enough weight. This also applies to the consumer discretionary sector.

Diversify by adding non-US companies

Most of the profitable companies with brand recognition and a global reach are in the US. But that does not mean that Europe, Africa, South America, and Asia don't have high-quality companies of their own, also. Sometimes you can find even better-undervalued companies outside of the USA. Instead of sticking to US companies, diversify your portfolio and go international.

I'm always careful when analyzing these companies because many companies overseas sell price-sensitive products, such as commodities or basic materials. I make sure to look for companies with a competitive advantage.

Many countries have been developing at a rapid pace these last decades, such as Brazil, Russia, India, China, and South Africa. Make sure to pay attention to taxes you would have to pay on dividends that you collect from countries outside of the US.

Table 6.4 List of Non-US Dividend Paying Companies

Ticker	Symbol
SSL	Sasol Limited
MBT	Mobil'nye Telesistemy
UL	Unilever
MTNOY	MTN Group Ltd
SRGHY	ShopRite Holdings
RDS	Royal Dutch Shell

I have noticed that countries outside of the US most of the time are lax with keeping a good dividend policy going. These companies might pay an increasing dividend for a couple of years and then cut the dividend.

I've also noticed that many companies pay dividends yearly or twice a year compared to the average quarterly dividend in the US. This is why I am also less strict when it comes to analyzing overseas companies.

Resources

There are quite a few resources online that are available for free when it comes to analyzing stocks. I've made a list of the ones I use the most:

Investopedia.com: Great resource for explaining many terms related to the stock market. They have helpful videos, also.

SeekingAlpha.com: Community of dividend investors who analyze and write articles about different companies.

Finviz.com: Great site to use for stock screening, stock research, and keeping up with different markets and currencies.

Morningstar.com: My go-to resource for financial statements, this site makes analyzing stocks so much easier.

Google Finance: I always have this site open; it gives me a quick overview of different companies' stock information and stock charts.

MSN Money: Similar to Google Finance, it has great graphs and stats.

Finance.yahoo.com: Similar to Google Finance, always good to check out, also.

Gurufocus.com: Good graph site for quickly checking earnings growth, dividend growth, payout ratio and more.

Dividend.com: Contains stock dividend information.

Stockcharts.com: Charting site used to track companies.

Below you will find how I quickly analyze a company step by step. The company we will look at is the Hershey Company.

What does the company do?
The Hershey Company (**HSY**) is the largest producer of chocolate and they sell their products worldwide. Hershey's been in existence for decades now, but they also have the right to produce and sell certain products such as Jolly Rancher, Kit Kat, Rolo, Twizzlers, and Payday.

Does the company have a sustainable long-term competitive advantage?
Hershey sells products that have built up their brand name. If you crave Kit Kat, there is no substitute; you have to buy Kit Kat. This also applies to the other products they sell, like their famous Hershey chocolate bars.

30 years from now, it's safe to say Hershey's will still be a chocolate confectionery, selling the same products they have for all these years.

Is the company in a position to grow?
Not only is Hershey's expanding their product line, but they also stay in the industry they are experts in. They also see future growth in South America and Asia.

Are the total revenue and earnings consistently growing?
Revenue has seen an average growth of 7% in the last 5 years and net income has seen growth also.

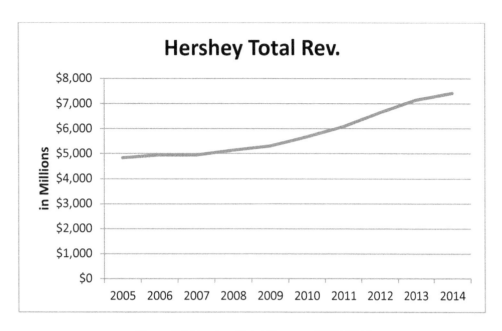

Figure 7.1 Hershey Total Revenue 2005-2014

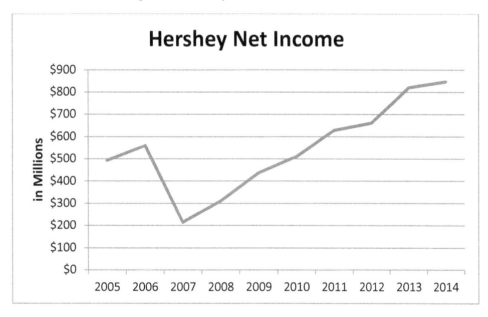

Figure 7.2 Hershey Net Income 2005-2014

How is the profit margin looking?

Profit margin has consistently been around 10% in the last 5 years and 9.23% in the last ten.

Is the ROE healthy? What about ROIC?

Both ROE and ROIC have been consistently looking great for the last 5 to 10 years (in the double digits).

Table 7.1 Hershey's ROE and ROIC

The Hershey Company	2010	2011	2012	2013	2014
Return on Equity %	62.83%	71.83%	70.10%	62.12%	55.36%
Return on Invested Capital %	22.86%	25.21%	25.46%	26.98%	25.01%

Is debt manageable?

Debt to Equity ratio for the last 5 years has been 1.48 and around 2 in the last year.

Total liabilities / Net income (before taxes) = $4,174,454,000 / $926,875,000 = 4.5. The company can pay all its debt (future interest expense excluded) in less than 5 years which is good.

Is the company buying back its stock?

Yes, Hershey has been buying back its stock, leaving fewer shares outstanding and increasing ownership for its owners.

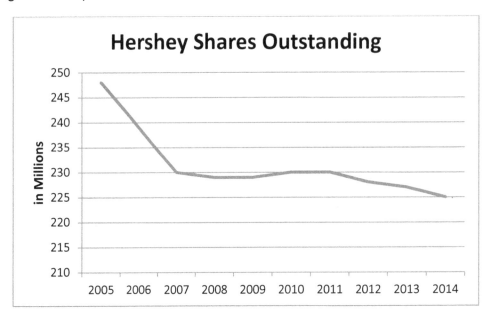

Figure 7.3 Hershey Stock Buyback 2005-2014

What's the dividend growth rate?

Hershey has been able to grow its dividend by around 11% in the last 5 years and over 9% in the last 10.

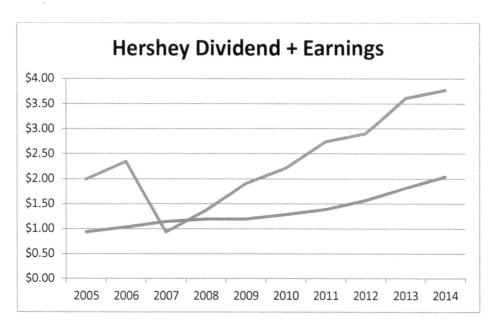

Figure 7.4 Hershey Earnings and Dividend 2005-2014

The bottom line is the dividend growth. 2009 was the only year the dividend didn't grow, it stayed at $1.19, but in 2010 it picked back up and saw an increase of 7.6%.

What is the dividend yield?
Right now, the dividend yield is 2.68%. The combination of a dividend yield higher than 2.5% and an annual growth rate averaging 11% in the last 5 years, makes this business a keeper.

What's the payout ratio?
The payout ratio has consistently been under 60%. It saw a huge spike in 2007 but was able to recover and stay under 60%. This shows me that management is hard at work keeping shareholders happy.

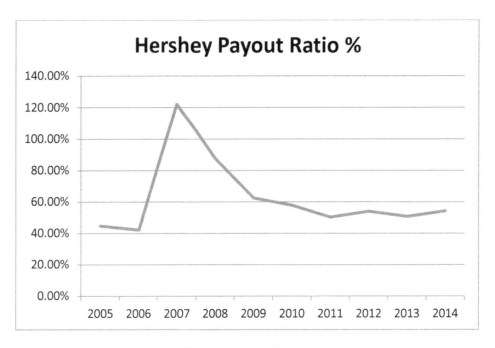

Figure 7.5 Hershey Payout Ratio 2005-2014

What is the P/E ratio?

P/E ratio is at 38.92. After the recent crash, the P/E ratio was bouncing between 20 and 25 for a couple of years and then spiked up close to 40. Normally I only buy companies when the P/E is 15 or below, but for Hershey, I'm willing to make an exception and buy at 20 times earnings (P/E = 20), or less.

For now, I will keep the Hershey Company on my **watch list** and buy whenever the P/E is lower; this should happen when there is a market correction or a crash.

Analyzing companies gets easier the more often you do it. You will also start to notice patterns with companies in the same industry.

Chapter Eight: Conclusion

This is the last chapter of the book, but it is the beginning of your journey to becoming a superhero. Superheroes possess extraordinary abilities and skills that leave the average human jealous, speechless, and in awe.

They also have the uncanny ability to stay calm, cool, and collected in the face of danger, while everybody else is panicking.

While doing their normal daily activities they might also blend in with the crowd and not stand out at all. But when duty calls, they can switch into superhero mode as fast as lightning.

Dividend investors are the superheroes of the investing community. They have the extraordinary skill to fly through cyberspace, analyze, buy, and sell different high-quality companies, without breaking a sweat. While doing this, they also receive **realized income** in the form of dividends, even when they are on vacation, working, or hibernating.

When the market crashes and everybody panics and starts to sell, the dividend superheroes stay calm, cool, and collected. And when the time is right, they kick it into awesome mode and achieve sensational feats that the average investor is too scared to undertake, leaving them baffled and scratching their heads afterward.

Dividend superheroes come in all shapes and sizes, from the lightest to the darkest hue. And last but not least, they have the remarkable ability of blending in.

Bonus: Investing in Yourself: Financial riches for a lifetime and beyond

Introduction: Vision for Success

The path to riches is waiting for you with open arms. Besides an overabundance of riches, wealth has additional benefits: financial freedom, peace of mind, no more long hours at work, exuberant lifestyle, and great health.

Why work your whole life stressing out over projects and unrealistic deadlines, horrible bosses, unqualified coworkers and all the irritants that present itself in corporate life, while you can take that same energy and work on creating wealth and ownership instead?

Not many people are able to generate wealth that can last them for a lifetime and beyond. Even many of our senior citizens who have worked their whole life and retired out of the job market have financial issues and distress.

Reason for this is that people focus on making money first and wealth secondary. The typical person focuses on working at a company and climbing up the corporate ladder or switching from one company to another every so often, getting a higher salary in the process.

While in the working years, people focus on all the essentials: a comfortable home in a great neighborhood, transportation to and from work, good school for their children, and their retirement account.

Nowadays, many people think that their home and retirement accounts are their wealth generators. But this is not how wealthy people think.

The secret to creating wealth is not through working for companies your whole life, but through assets acquired from the three **wealth builders**.

Chapter One: Wealth Creation

Stop working for money and start working towards acquiring assets! Now, don't get me wrong, money plays an important role in building wealth, but if you only focus on making money, you will never see the bigger picture.

An asset is something of **value that you own**. As a smart investor we're only going to focus on assets that appreciate in value. A car for example is an asset that depreciates in value (unless it's a classic and you work on the upkeep), because it is worth less the more miles you put on it by driving it around.

Not only are we going to focus on appreciating assets, we'll also use these specific assets for their **increasing income streams**. However, not all assets produce an income stream.

Wealthy people continuously acquire assets. This is how they keep getting wealthier and because there is no retirement date for wealth, like there is for a career, they keep acquiring assets until they pass away. Their wealth is then strategically passed down to their family.

Warren Buffet, the third wealthiest person on this planet, and his partner Charlie Munger are over 85 years old, still working on acquiring assets.

Wealthy vs rich

Do not confuse wealthy individuals for rich ones. Wealth is always acquired through assets. An NFL player making $20 million is rich, but does not own any assets.

Also, you can be a high-income earner, but if you are drowning in debt, you are not even close to being wealthy.

For example, a Vice President of Sales who works for a Fortune 500 company makes a salary of $1.4 million a year. He or she is rich, but has a debt amount that totals $3.6 million. This person needs to seriously take a look at his or her expenses and make some major adjustments.

When I mention wealth, I'm talking about owning valuable assets beyond your debt. Wealth that produces income for you even when you do not have to put in any labor.

Working for money

When you work for money, the amount you can make is limited by your skills. The more knowledge and skills you acquire, the more you're worth to your company and you could potentially make more money.

That's why someone working a fast food job or as a sales associate at your local clothing store does not make a healthy income. The skills required to do such jobs are basic and you don't even need any type of education. Most of the time you do not even get any training, you just start working on the floor your first day on the job.

You are also easily replaceable by anybody and everybody.

People with specialized skills are not as easily replaceable and can demand and negotiate a higher salary. For example, computer programmers, lawyers, and doctors.

Working for money is also limited by your physical health. Once you get terribly ill, or you cannot physically work anymore, the money you were making stops coming in, because you cannot use your labor in exchange for money anymore.

The corporate ladder

The typical middle-class family focuses on climbing the corporate ladder. Spending time building up the company they work for, focusing on realizing the owners dream for the company. Instead, they should be working on their own dream of financial freedom.

While climbing the corporate ladder, you'll be given more responsibilities, work, stress, and less free time, every time you get promoted to a higher position. This is a catch 22, in order to make more money you will have to give up something. This could be time you could spend with your family or your sanity, because stress will peak it's ugly head.

While putting all your time and effort in the company, you'll also setup a retirement account with the company and put substantially less thought in it compared to your daily tasks at work.

When you just start your career, retirement is the last thing on your mind. However, it needs to be the first thing on your list of things to get serious about if you are young, because you have time on your side. Time for your investments to grow.

The sooner you start the less you would have to invest in order to reach your retirement goals.

If your retirement goal is to reach $1 million. Starting at the age of 24, you would only have to invest a little over $370 a month to reach your goal at age 65 (with an average 7% growth rate).

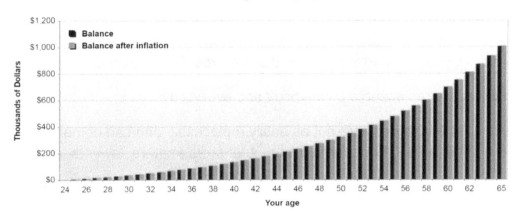

Figure 1.1 Retirement goal – Source Dinkytown.net

However, if you started investing at the age of 40, you would need to play catch up and invest $1,300 a month to reach your $1 million goal at age 65.

With age comes an increasingly urgent feeling for security and that is when retirement is taken more seriously. Most of the time people start thinking about their retirement when it's too late and they have to start playing catch up.

This happens in their late 40s, early 50s. They can see 60 on the horizon and know that there aren't many more working years left before retirement. It's also at this time when your health can become a serious issue and age discrimination is taking place in the job market.

Working for assets

There are only three vehicles that allow you to acquire assets to build wealth:

- Business
- Real Estate
- Stock market

Interestingly enough, most of us are, to a certain extent, familiar with these three vehicles. Chances are you already have a retirement account setup at your job with investments in the stock market. You might own or rent a home, so you know the basics of real estate and you already work for a business, so you have some knowledge about business models.

In order to become wealthy off of these three wealth builders, you need to change the way in which you interact with them.

Instead of working for a company, you need to create or buy your own company. Instead of being a tenant, you need to become the landlord. Instead of giving your money to a greedy/shady investment banker and crossing your fingers for the better or only investing your money in index funds, you need educate yourself and start buying your own stocks.

You are supposed to own valuable assets that create a passive income stream. This is different from **earned income**. Which is money you only receive in exchange for labor.

The goal is to turn earned income into passive income from assets. How you use these wealth builders will either leave you broke, rich or wealthy.

If you jump in and try to create wealth without any knowledge, you will lose your shirt and end up broke. Many people have been scammed by investing their hard-earned money into unknown businesses or in the stock market not knowing they got bamboozled until it was too late.

If you use these wealth builders only to create earned income, you could become rich but not wealthy, like someone flipping houses for a profit, only working for companies, or someone day trading for a living.

Lastly, if you convert these wealth builders into assets, you increase your chances of becoming wealthy.

Ownership is key

When I mention assets, the focus is on ownership. When you work on collecting assets you are working on owning something of value that you can pass down to your family. Ownership of the right assets also gets you closer to financial freedom.

When you work for a company, your primary reason for being there is the money you are earning. There are additional benefits of course, like social connections, a feeling of belonging to a group and learning skills that might benefit you on your career path.

However, money is still the primary reason you work for a company, everything else is just a benefit that comes with the job.

Imagine being at a job interview and you are told that you won't get paid, but the company has really fun social activities and you will get to meet nice people. You would probably get up and leave thinking they must be crazy.

The problem with working for a company is that you cannot pass your job down to your family.

Collecting or creating assets that can sustain your lifestyle will start out as a slow learning process and there is risk involved, but if you stick with it you will have more personal abundance compared to working for someone else.

The essence of time

Money comes and goes and assets can be bought or sold, but **time is finite**. The amount of time you have is literally limited to your time on this earth. To make matters even more interesting, we don't have a clue how much time we have left.

Some would even say time is more valuable than what you own. You need to make time work in your favor. Ever heard of the saying time flies or where has the time gone. If you go through life one day at a time never planning for your future, time will catch up to you eventually, and you'll be talking about all the things you should've done while you were younger and still had the time.

But if you own valuable assets, time is on your side, because with time you gain more assets or the assets that you own increase in value. As time passes, your assets create you more wealth.

Chapter Two: Wealth builder #1 - Business

Many entrepreneurs have been able to build their wealth fast with their business, whether it is an online or a brick and mortar business.

Just look at some of the wealthiest people on the planet, like Elon Musk, Jeff Bezos and Larry Ellison.

Elon Musk has created and sold many successful businesses. A large portion of his wealth comes from his current company Tesla, which creates electric vehicles and solar energy systems.

His company is worth over $50 billion.

Jeff Bezos, creator of Amazon.com, had an idea back in the early nineties. His idea was to set up an ecommerce store where you could buy books online after he noticed that physical stores where limited by the physical space of the store. His online store would not have this limitation.

However, he quickly learned that he was limiting his store by only selling books, so he opened up his online store to sell just about everything else. Right now, his company is worth over $500 billion.

Larry Ellison created Oracle, a software business that created the relational databases we use every day and most of us don't even know it, because it is the underlying technological infrastructure that powers most of our daily activities, from the cell phones that we use to swiping your credit card and more.

The Oracle corporation is worth over $200 billion.

As you can see, the sky is the limit when it comes to how creative you can be with starting your own business and the amount of money you can generate.

You can start small as a one-man team, by offering lawn mowing services or snow shoveling.

You can go the online route and start selling products online through Shopify, information products or services through lead generation.

If you have more capital to work with you could start a franchise fast food chain, healthy food or even fitness centers.

There are many options available when you start your own business. There are also many tax benefits with setting up a business.

Many small entrepreneurs start their business as a sole proprietary and once they start to get the ball rolling they incorporate it into the flexible Limited Liability Corporation (LLC).

The steps to making your business work is to only focus on what you are good at and outsource or automate everything else. The last thing you want to do is work on your business 24/7 not allowing you to enjoy the fruit of your labor.

For example, you start your own online e-commerce drop shipping website. You've done the research on which platform to use, the products you are going to sell and how to advertise it.

You are excellent at coming up with unique products to sell and love analyzing your revenue and expense reports.

You are severely lacking in creativity and coding skills. You are good with data analysis, but bad at coding ecommerce website, graphic design and online marketing.

You could outsource your web development; hire both a great graphic designer and a digital media buyer, which will allow you to focus on analyzing your website's performance.

It is extremely important that your business involves something you are interested and believe in. If you don't believe in your own business, no one else will.

Also, if you aren't interested or passionate about your business, it will fail. You will be spending many hours alone working on your business, so it's best to choose a business venture you have some interest in.

Many starting entrepreneurs fail a couple of times before they are successful. Their past failures are used as a learning experience on what not to do for the next business idea.

You also want to stay away from being a one-man team. It's fine to start out by yourself, but you need to keep expansion in mind, by adding more employees.

A physician who has a private practice is a one-man team. If he takes a vacation, gets sick or even passes away, the whole business is at a standstill. Planning is of the essence before you decide on what type of business you want to run.

Chapter Three: Wealth Builder #2 - Real Estate

It's no secret that many wealthy individuals attained their riches through real estate. It's an old, but stable method which will increase your wealth. Play it in your favor and you can set it up to not take much time away from your daily activities.

There are many benefits to setting up a real estate empire. If you do it the right way you can attain financial freedom, while still growing your empire. Not only do you gain valuable skills, you also make valuable connections in the real estate world, which will be able to help you on your journey.

Investors can create wealth in real estate through income properties. This allows you to collect rent payments from your tenants. Your rent payments should increase with time, due to cost of living increases or improvements that you make to the properties. Also, the more properties you own, the more rent payments you will collect.

If you need to pay off your bank loan, the rent payments that you collect are used to pay down the mortgage, so the tenant is actually helping you in paying down debt, but also the taxes and insurance.

With debt pay down, your equity in the property grows and once you pay off the mortgage, you own the property free and clear.

Properties to focus on: commercial real estate, apartment complexes, strip malls, hotels, single family homes, duplexes, triplexes and quads.

For investors just starting out it's recommended to begin with duplexes, triplexes or quads. Why? Because it costs considerably less money to buy these properties.

If you get your numbers right they will cash flow nicely and in general it's also easier to fill a duplex with a tenant compared to finding a business that wants to rent space in your commercial property.

Wealth creation in real estate is through accumulating income properties that cash flow. This means you are generating a cash distribution from your investment.

If you plan on making around $400 on average in net cash flow from an income property, you can do the math to project out your financial freedom number.

So, if you want to make $100k a year with real estate, you would need around 20-21 income properties, which will generate a little over $8,000 in net cash flow, to reach this goal. Once you pay off the mortgage on these properties, your monthly income will jump even higher.

Many people who jump into the real estate market try to flip houses. This is a good way to make money, but as a smart investor we want to acquire appreciating assets that pay us income.

Flipping houses can be a lot of work, because you need to scout the market for homes on sale, buy them below value, renovate and then sell again. This leaves you back at square one with some money in your pocket, but no asset.

What about working as a real estate agent? There's nothing wrong with making earned income, which is money that you have to work for, being your own boss as a real estate agent and making good money in the process. But as a real estate agent, you are still not acquiring any assets.

As a smart investor, we only work for assets. And we only sell assets once they don't generate any meaningful income for us.

So, in real estate it's recommended to buy properties below market value and generate income consistently through rent payments, which would be your cash flow.

Leverage Money

A big advantage of real estate is that you can leverage other people's time and money for your investments.

If there is a property available on the market for $100k, you don't have to save up that total amount to purchase the property. You can use other people's money. If you deal with a bank, you would only have to put 20% down, which is $20k, and the bank will loan you the other $80k. Or if you are willing to live in your property and it is your first home, you could use an FHA loan, which only requires you to put 3.5% down.

Let's say you wanted to buy a duplex, live in one side and rent out the other, for $150,000. With an FHA (Federal Housing Administration) loan you would only have to come up with $5,250 for the down payment. The rest would be the loan amount you would borrow from the bank, so $144,750.

Keep in mind, however, that you will also have to fork up some money for the closing cost and PMI (private mortgage insurance).

Bank's motive

The bank does not lend you money out of the kindness of their heart. The bank is in business to make money. So, if the bank lends you $80k on a $100k property, on a 30-year mortgage at 4%, you end up paying the bank $140k for the life of the loan.

Why does the bank require you to put some money down, because they want you to have some skin in the game. By putting down 20% down, the bank is already in a good spot. If you default on your $80k loan on a property worth $100k, the bank will take ownership. Even if they sell the property for $90k, they still made $10k profit (taxes not taken into account), because they got it for $80k.

Other ways to get loans

You could also strike a deal with private lenders to get a loan for them. By being creative you can come up with ways on how to put less money down or no money at all to acquire your income property.

You should also use other people's time/skills to help you in real estate. You are just one person who cannot do everything, from keeping up with local tenant laws to knowing how to fix plumbing issues; you will have limited knowledge in one or more areas.

It's recommended to hire the right people with the right credentials to make your life easier.

Leveraging People's Time

Having a team of experts cuts down your learning curve tremendously. It also saves you time from having to figure everything out on your own. Some experts you want to have on your team: real estate agents, property managers, mortgage brokers, attorneys, mentors and contractors.

Keep Credit in Check

Before you even think about buying a property, you need to make sure your credit score is error free and as high as you can get it. Companies like CreditWise and CreditKarma allow you to see your credit score for free and what you can do to improve it.

Some common practices you need to keep in mind when dealing with your credit score:

- Pay all your bills on time
- Keep your credit card utilization under 10% of your total available credit
- Average age of your credit accounts (higher is better)
- Total credit accounts (closed accounts, also)
- Hard inquiries should be limited

Tip: I always try to increase my credit card limit every 6 months and only use a fraction of my available credit. Banks like to see that you can handle your credit responsibly.

Only using a small amount of your available credit and paying it off on time, will boost your credit score.

Once you know your credit is up to par, it should be at least 600, you can then get a loan unless you will finance the purchase 100%, which is uncommon. If you go to a bank, they will pull your credit, look over your financial balance sheet (your debt vs assets) to determine what you qualify for.

The bank will allow you to choose between a multitude of loans: FHA loans, VA loans, 30-year fixed rate, 15-year balloon rate, etc. If possible, FHA or VA loans are good to go with, but if not available, stick with the 30-year fixed rate loan with the option to pay it off early.

The 30-year fix rate gives you lower payments and they are fixed over the life of the loan. Once you start buying more properties, the bank more than likely won't allow you to get this loan.

Getting Started

You have to be familiar with the market you buy real estate in. A real estate agent can help you with pulling comps of recently sold properties, which means they will look at comparable properties that recently sold. Or you can do some digging of your own by using sites like redfin.com, zillow.com, and homes.com.

You should also know how safe the areas are where you want to purchase real estate. Crimereports.com lets you check the crime in your location

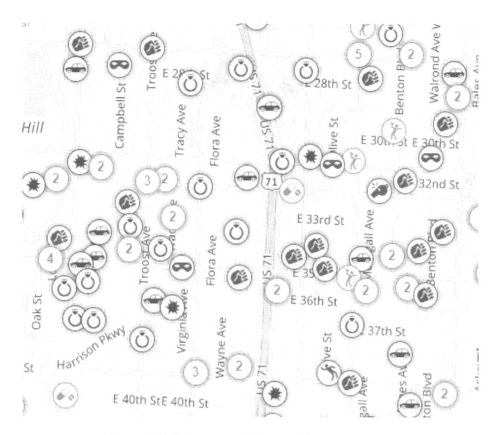

Figure 3.1 Crime map – Source Crimereports.com

You also need to know how much rent is charged in that area. Rentometer.com and craigslist.com are good starting points. Talking to a property manager or even real estate agent can also help you with the rent numbers.

Figure 3.2 Local area rent – Source Craigslist.com

How much rent is charged depends on the home market value, the area where the property is located, and how many rooms are available. A 3 bedroom house with 2 bathrooms will rent for a higher amount than a 2 bedroom with only 1 bathroom if the properties are in the same location.

Figure 3.3 Average rent – Source Rentometer.com

Doing the numbers

If you figure out what the monthly rent is you will be receiving, you can project how much net profit you could get. For this example, you want to cash flow around $300 per month.

A duplex is listed at $105,000. After pulling some comps you know that the fair market value of the property is $95,000. After some negotiations you were able to push the purchase price to $85,000 (the seller wanted to sell fast, because she is planning on reinvesting the proceeds from the sale into a different venture).

You also got the rent roll (documented monthly rent the landlord receives), which is $600 per door per month. So, the landlord is receiving $1,200 a month in rental income.

You're planning on putting 20% down on purchasing the property and the bank will finance the rest. Your down payment would be $17,100 and the bank will finance $68,400 (add these two up and you get the $85,000 purchase price).

At $68,400 and a 4% interest rate, your monthly mortgage payment is $326.55 on a 30/yr fixed rate loan.

You have some operating expenses that you need to budget for, also. Property management fees, leasing cost, maintenance reserves, capital expenditures, property taxes, insurance and any other expenses such as HOA.

After adding them all up your total expenses come up to $472.75 per month.

To calculate your Net Operating Income, you take your Net Rental Income – Total Expenses.

The Net Rental Income is slightly different from your Rental Income. You always want to account for vacancies. At a 5% vacancy rate, your $1,200 in Net Rental Income will come down to $1,140.

Your Net Operating Income (NOI) = $667.25 ($1,140 - $472.75). The NOI never includes your mortgage payment.

So, the next step is to calculate your Net Cash Flow., which is your NOI – Mortgage Payment. $667.25 - $326.55 (mortgage payment).

Your Net Cash Flow is $340.75

Let's continue by calculating your Cash-on-cash return and Cap rate.

Your Cash-on-cash return lets you know how much return you are initially getting from your investment. You calculate this by dividing your yearly Net Cash Flow by the total amount of cash you put in to purchase the property, including repairs and your closing cost.

Your yearly net cash flow is $4,088.38 ($340.70 * 12 months) and your Total Cash In is $17,100 (down payment) + $4,000 (closing cost) + $5,000 (repairs) = $26,100

Your Cash-on-cash return = $4,088.38 / $26,000 = 15.7%

Investors like to use the CoC return to compare how they stack up against other investments, like stocks or bonds.

If you would make an 8% return on your stocks and only 5% on bonds, then this real estate investment at 15.7% is a better deal.

Your Capitalization Rate, or just Cap Rate, is the ratio of NOI to the property's purchase price. Investors use this calculation to quickly get an answer of how their investment compares to the average. For income properties an average cap rate of 10% (or higher) is the goal.

The Cap Rate on this investment is = $8,007 (yearly NOI) / $85,000 (purchase price) = 9.4%. Not quite 10% yet, but still close and most investors would take this deal.

Doing your due diligence

You've scoped out a good location, ran the numbers and like what you are seeing. Your net cash flow should always be in the green.

You are ready to place an offer, put in the necessary clauses and have an inspection and appraisal done. These are a necessary evil you don't want to skip out on. It's also advised to be present and take notes for the inspection walk through.

There will be some back and forth during this process, but if all goes well you just bought your first (or second property). Time to pop some champagne!!

Chapter Four: Wealth Builder #3 – Investing

Stock market investing is the last tried and true method of generating and maintaining wealth. The most common method of making money on the stock market is buy low and sell high.

However, we are only going to focus on buying stocks in high quality dividend paying companies that are trading at a discount.

Dividends are money paid to shareholders by the companies that they own shares in. Companies pay out dividends out of their earnings. However, not all companies pay out a dividend.

Why focus on high quality dividend paying companies? Because the dividend income provides a stable source of income that keeps growing year after year and if you reinvest your dividend income into purchasing more whole or partial shares, you will end up generating even more dividend income.

PepsiCo pays $2.96 in dividend income. Buy 50 shares and you will receive $148 in dividend income.

This might not seem like a lot of money, but with time on your side and continuously buying more shares, you will increase your wealth.

In the image below, you can see what your dividend income might look like from PepsiCo if the company keeps increasing the dividend by 8.3% every year and you keep reinvesting the dividends (this is without buying any additional shares).

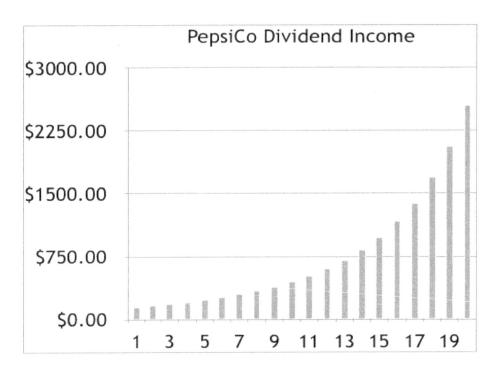

Figure 4.1 PepsiCo dividend income

Now, PepsiCo is just one company, imagine if you owned 40-50 high quality dividend paying stocks. Your yearly dividend income would be in the six figures.

The dividend companies you need to have on your watch list should be companies that have an easy to understand business model, have a competitive advantage, are positioned for growth with a consistent profit margin, manageable debt, and increase their dividend faster than the rate of inflation in the past ten years. They also need to have a low payout ratio and a good return on equity (ROE). This information can be retrieved from the company's annual report.

Let's look at an example, the company Ross Stores is one that would check all the boxes.

Ross Stores (ROST) owns and operates retail stores offering very affordable apparel and home fashion across the United States. They also operate dd's Discounts. Savings range from 20-60% compared to department stores.

This is also where Ross Stores' competitive advantage lies, you can visit any of their stores and be amazed at name brand merchandise selling considerably cheaper than the more well-known department stores.

Ross Stores is also in a very good position to grow. They are present in 36 states and are continuously opening up new stores.

Ross Stores have also increased their revenue at 8% on average these past ten years.

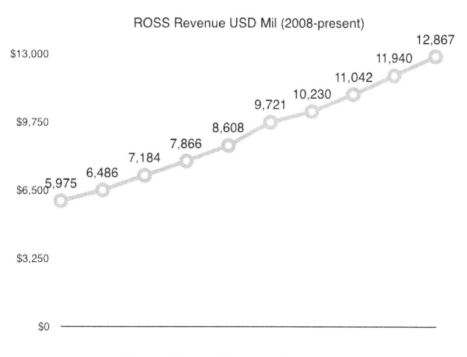

Figure 4.2 Ross Stores yearly revenue

Ross has been able to grow their Net Income by about 16% on average these last 10 years. They have been able to keep their profit margin consistent at 8% the past 5 years.

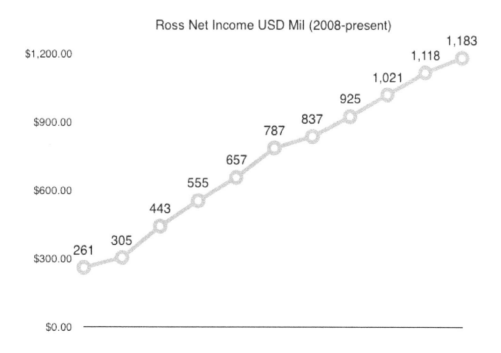

Figure 4.3 Ross Store net income

With an increase in net income and earnings, Ross has also been able to increase their dividend payout nicely, at around 16% the last five years, while keeping the payout ratio low, at around 20%.

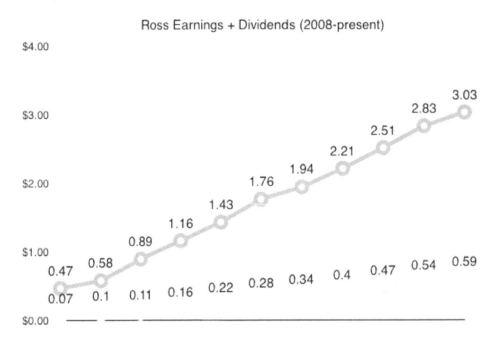

Figure 4.4 Ross Stores earnings and dividend payments

A company pays out dividends out of its earnings, so growing earnings year over year, positions the company to also increase its dividends. That's why it's very important that companies you analyze increase their performance metrics every year.

Ross Stores has also done a great job managing their debt. Looking at their total liabilities and comparing it to their net income (before taxes), Ross Stores is able to pay off their total debt within 2 years.

Ross Stores also buys back their own shares. It's important to see if a company does this, because if they do, that means there are less shares available on the market. These shares will be retired, which in turn increases the per share value of the company.

Right now, Ross Stores has a market capitalization of $28 billion (market cap means what the company is worth). There are 385.59 million shares outstanding, which means there are that many shares available on the market to buy and sell.

$28 billion / 385.59 million shares = $72.61 (share price). Let's say you own 10 stocks in Ross. Your investment is worth $726.10 (10 stocks x $72.61 share price).

Hypothetically speaking, if the company bought half of all the shares there would only be 192.79 million shares left to trade. The company is still worth $28 billion, but now your investment is worth $1452.20 (double).

Companies, however, don't go about buying that many shares back. Ross, however, has been buying back its shares, leaving less shares on the market for shareholders.

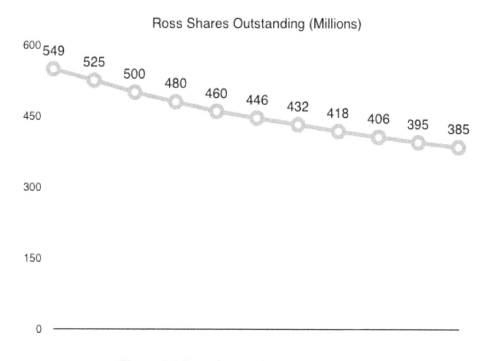

Figure 4.5 Ross Stores shares outstanding

A list of other great companies to keep an eye on and to analyze:

- McDonalds
- Coca Cola
- Fastenal
- Flower Foods
- PepsiCo Inc.
- T. Rowe Price Group
- Realty Income
- 3M Company
- Unilever
- Nike
- Lowe's Companies
- Kimberly-Clark Corporation
- Procter & Gamble
- Clorox Company

- Estee Lauder Companies

These are all great leading companies in their respective fields that have stood the test of time and they all pay increasing dividends. To find additional companies, think about the products you use on a daily basis and see if these pay out a dividend. You would be surprised at which ones do.

The previous list of dividend paying companies grow their dividend every single year, without you having to do anything but hold onto your investment.

In the image below, you can see that Nike has been able to grow their dividend by about 9-16% every year over the last ten years, even during our economic crisis in 2008-2009.

Table 4.1 Nike dividend growth rate

	2008	2009	2010	2011	2012	2013	2014	2015	2016	2017
Nike Dividends USD	$0.22	$0.24	$0.27	$0.30	$0.35	$0.41	$0.47	$0.54	$0.62	$0.70
Dividend Growth %	9.09%	12.50%	11.11%	16.67%	17.14%	14.63%	14.89%	14.81%	12.90%	

Now, ask yourself if the company that you work for gives you a 13% raise each year.

You should reinvest the dividend income to buy more shares and continue to add more money to your account to purchase shares. The savvy investor will use income generated from their business and/or real estate properties to invest in the stock market.

The goal is to generate enough dividend income to live off, so your dividend checks allow you to retire early.

Of course, there are other methods to make money in the stock market, like day trading, this is where you buy and sell stocks for a profit within one day, selling short, penny stocks, FOREX, commodity and high frequency trading.

These all require work, you only own them for a short amount of time (because you are constantly buying and selling) and most don't pay a dividend. As a smart investor we focus on ownership of assets that pay us an increasing income, that's why we don't focus on these methods of generating income.

However, there is nothing wrong with these methods. Many investors make great money with them and then switch over to a more passive dividend income strategy.

Tip: Four good brokerage firms to get you to start investing in the stock market:

- Ally.com
- TDAmeritrade

- E*Trade
- Interactive Brokers

Chapter Five: Old Money vs New Money

You can consider the tried and true methods of building wealth old money, because they have stood the test of time when it comes to dependability on maintaining wealth. Stocks and real estate are old money. There are generations of families that inherited fortunes wrapped in old money.

Why are real estate and the stock market considered to be old money?

Real estate is all around us to monetize, the building you are working in, your home, and the land that you walk or drive on, and the stores or restaurants you visit.

The stock market is old money, because it's used by wealthy individuals and institutions to park their money, where it can keep growing. There will always be a need for a place to park excess amount of wealth.

New money on the other hand is wealth created in this new age, but the future on this sustainability is still up in the air. Many tech businesses fall under this category.

Web 2.0 companies like Twitter and Facebook are new money. With a cash inflow of angel investors, these companies took off and are still going strong. But how long and how sustainable these business models are is still to be seen.

A company like Myspace pretty much came and went. I like to stick with the business models of the old money. Also, many entrepreneurs and business owners who create their wealth from new money, turn around and invest all or a portion of their wealth in old money, like Bill Gates.

He is the co-founder of the successful company Microsoft, when he retired he invested a lion share of his money in his holding company Cascade Investment.

Time to start creating wealth

You should start your journey as soon as possible. The entrepreneur spirit is particularly alive in our youngest generation. Also, when you are young, you have time on your side to make mistakes, learn from them and still bounce back.

You can definitely be an entrepreneur in your older years, like Colonel Sanders from KFC. But the older we get; our life priorities change and most of us lose our zest for adventure and risk taking.

If you are lucky, you might have a family member that started you on your path to wealth building by buying you a stock in a dividend paying company, allowing you to follow how your stock is doing on the market and receive a dividend every quarter.

With companies laying off their employees due to outsourcing, automation and robotics, the world can always use smart young entrepreneurs who can change the world with their bright ideas.

Chapter Six: Maintaining Wealth

It takes time to create wealth. It does not happen overnight, you have to plan for it and set goals. Once you have your goals in place, it takes consistency and determination to reach those goals.

Maintaining your wealth could be even harder than creating it. The business landscape can change on a whim, economies can crash, customers could lose interest in your products or you could just be a lawsuit away from going bankrupt. Many things can and will go wrong, so it's very important to also focus on maintaining your wealth.

Managing business

In order to maintain your business, you have to be able to delegate and only focus on the tasks that you like doing and are good at doing.

Delegating allows you to take your business to the next level by hiring the right personnel. This frees up your time, allowing you to have a life outside of work and enjoy your riches.

Besides delegating specific business tasks, you should also automate and outsource.

Hiring the right personnel will always be a big challenge. Not only do you need to hire the right people for the job, you also need to compensate them fairly and have additional company perks, like flexible workdays, to make them feel at home.

Making sure to hire the right people also puts you in a position to expand your business and if you want to take it to the next level you can turn it from a private company into a public one by getting it on the stock market.

Listing your company on the stock market or going public has its pros and cons.

The company can raise capital, with an IPO, to inject back into the business. It also puts the company in the public market and creates a sense of accomplishment and recognition for employees' hard work.

Cons are that there will be pressure from outside forces such as stakeholders or shareholder's on how the company should conduct itself.

There are different examples of companies that started as a mom and pop shop and they expanded and went public, like Walmart. Do not neglect humble beginnings.

To keep your company competitive, you need to be able to generate consistent revenue which increases year over year, increase profit margins, or cut costs. It's extremely important to have the right person manage the company books.

Managing Real Estate

Managing properties should be done by property managers. A good property manager will make your life easy and allow you to sleep peacefully at night. They will handle all tenant questions and complaints. They also know good contractors who will fix, repair or rebuild your property. They also collect rent and evict nonpaying tenants.

Make sure to interview multiple property managers to get a good idea of who you want to partner up with. You can get good referrals from your real estate agent or doing a quick search online. You can also find some good mentors at local real estate clubs, which could refer you to their property managers.

Most property managers will take 8-12% of your gross rent. Some will also need to get paid a leasing cost and/or all or some of the first month's rent. So, make sure to meet with multiple PMs before you make a decision.

It's fairly doable to manage 1, 2, or 3 properties on your own, especially if you are the handy man type. But the more properties you add to your portfolio, the more time consuming it will be to manage them.

It goes without saying, but you (or your property manager) need to listen to your tenant's complaints and make them feel welcome and at home, you don't want to have the reputation of being known as a slumlord.

Focusing on cash flow in Real Estate is not a make money fast game. It takes time to build your cash flowing income portfolio. With every income producing asset you acquire, you're moving closer to financial freedom. The knowledge and connections you gain will be valuable to take your wealth to the next level.

The more properties you buy and loans you are applying for, your debt ratio will go up. If you have too much debt in the form of mortgage loans, banks will be hesitant to give out additional loans for you to buy other properties. You hit this ceiling when you have around 4-10 properties.

This is when you have to either pay down your existing loans or do some creative financing. Private lending or portfolio lending are some of your options.

Once you are a couple of years into Real Estate investing, you can take your experience, connections and generated income and start buying commercial properties or even transition into franchising. Having a good accountant or accounting system will become a necessity.

Stock Investing Management

While you are growing your portfolio of dividend paying stocks, you need to keep an eye on the businesses you have bought stock in and you also need to pay attention to the dividend payments that you get.

If you have bought shares in 30-50 companies, you should read the annual report of the companies every year they come out. In the buying phase you already did the research by analyzing the company's performance and how the company makes money with its business model.

For example, a company like Flower Foods (FLO) produces bakery products it supplies to warehouses and directly to stores.

Another example of an easy business model to understand is, Nike. The company designs, creates, markets, and sells athletic apparel worldwide.

It's very important to only buy shares in companies you understand. If a company's business model changes, you should be alert, because with change comes a lot of uncertainty in a company's revenue and expenses.

It's fine if a company expands its business by buying out their competitors, but it can become a problem if a company ventures into a totally different market.

For example, Mondelez International, one of the world's largest snack companies, tried to buyout the Hershey Company, which is America's largest chocolate manufacturing company.

The buyout was unsuccessful, but Mondelez stayed in their own lane trying to buy a company in their market.

Now, if a company like Microsoft wanted to get into the gum manufacturing business, it would raise many red flags, because that is a totally different business compared to the software business Microsoft is in.

When companies also take these types of actions, it brings up questions to their existing business model. Is it still relevant? Can it produce increasing revenue? Why would they have to go into a different business?

Your dividend stream

While you own these stocks, you will receive dividends on a frequent basis (mostly quarterly). As long as you continue to receive dividends that keep up or grow faster than inflation, which is 3.5%, your money contains its buying power.

These dividend paying companies are inflation averse and you need to keep them in your portfolio.

The only reason to sell these stocks is if they cut or eliminate their dividend. During the financial crisis of 2008, a slew of companies that pay out dividends ended up on the chopping block.

A big-name company like General Electric ended up cutting its dividend in half. The list of companies I presented earlier have not gone through this decline.

Even during the recession, they were able to increase their dividend payout. These are the types of companies you need to focus on to put on your watch list and buy when the time is right.

Chapter Seven: Wait! Don't Fall for These Traps

On your journey to wealth there are many traps you need to avoid. We will discuss the six most common ones.

Jump in without any knowledge

It's really easy to get hyped about a new business idea or real estate purchase and take a leap of faith.

You need to have at least some basic knowledge of what you are getting yourself into. Reading this book is a start, but I highly encourage you to also find mentors, read books, listen to seminars, etc. Do not get bogged down by information overload, but do get some basic knowledge

Being scatter brained

A lack of focus will hurt your progress. It's very important to redirect your energy to focus on a specific goal like a laser beam.

This will allow your brain to come up with creative ways to solve problems when you hit a road block. If you constantly jump around trying out new ideas you will spread yourself too thin and only become frustrated.

Take things for granted

There is nothing wrong with dreaming about your future and how your life should be. But every once in a while, you should also enjoy what you have already accomplished in life. This will give you the mental energy to move forward and try out new ideas.

Advice from the wrong people

Sometimes people that mean you no harm could give you some bad advice. Taking the world in your own hands and taking entrepreneurial steps can be quite scary.

People close to you do not want to see you fail, so they might discourage you from taking risks. That's why it's very important that you believe in what you are doing, because if you are not confident in your own decisions, no one else will be.

Not keeping an eye on your numbers

In any business venture or investment that you get into, you need to always pay attention to your numbers. This could be your revenue metrics, real estate calculations, etc.

Starting out it's always best if you can do the numbers before you hire someone else to do this for you.

Not having fun

Love what you do, do what you love. If what you do does not excite you, it will just be a drag and you won't give it your all. Failure and frustration will be common, but if you have a passion or even like what you do, you will have a more enjoyable experience while giving it your all.

Chapter Eight: Conclusion

Starting the process of thinking about wealth and then taking the necessary steps to plan and reach your goals are what will set you apart from the average Joe.

The road will not be easy, but it will be fulfilling. Keep in mind that you are not the first person who has decided to take matters into your own hands, by focusing on your future by building generational wealth.

Use this book as a reference guide and even motivation if you feel that you need that extra push to get started or keep you on the right path.

Stick to your goals and hesitation and possible frustration will turn into joy and exuberance.

9 781087 802251